FEARONOMICS

A Stimulus of Hope for Tough Economic Times

Dr. Bill Moore

Harrison House

Tulsa, OK

14 13 12 11   10 9 8 7 6 5 4 3 2 1

Fearonomics: A Stimulus of Hope for Tough Economic Times
ISBN 13: 978-1-60683-309-4
ISBN 10: 1-60683-309-X

Copyright © by Bill Moore
350 West 802
Brownsville, TX 89520

Published by Harrison House LLC
P.O. Box 35035
Tulsa, OK 74153

www.harrisonhouse.com

CONTENTS

DEDICATION

To my loving wife, Anne, who never lets me give up and always tells me my stuff is good even when it's not. You are a constant voice of faith concerning our own personal finances. You remain my inspiration as we approach twenty-five incredible years of marriage. I love you, babe— you're the greatest. To Livingway Family Church, whose members allow me the freedom to work on projects like this book and are willing to share Anne and me with the rest of the body of Christ. Church, it's a joy to serve you.

Introduction

Sometime in the fall of 2008 it hit me—the reality of the economy and the sense of fear that troubled so many people. It was tangible. It was a force to be reckoned with. It was real. There was definitely a sense of desperation among the people. I began to find myself thinking, *Conserve. Pull back. Play it safe. Save up. These are troublesome times. How will we survive?*

We must be reminded that we are not survivors—we are more than conquerors. It's amazing how, in the heat of the battle, we forget our true identity. It's also amazing how quickly fear can grip our hearts. Like an armed robber, fear steps into our world, and everything else fades to the background. This was definitely an emotion I haven't felt for quite some time. It seemed like years since I had been afraid of anything. When I was small, some friends played a trick on me and locked me in a walk-in cooler. Now *that* was fear, and to this day I have a strong dislike for small, tight spaces. However, the spirit of fear descending on our society, which has been fueled by the news media, is real, and many people are struggling just to keep a positive attitude.

I decided to pray about this spirit of fear in the early part of December 2008. During this prayer time, I felt a change in my spirit as the Lord began to move in my heart. It was as if faith had hit me from the top of my head to the soles of my feet. It was then that faith came alive within me, and I realized I should be part of the solution and not a part of the problem. I realized that we needed to go back to the Scriptures and pay attention to the great plan God has for us.

We focus on the faithfulness of God: how He will never leave us nor forsake us, even to the ends of the earth. God let me know it was time for us to use our faith and not accept all of the negative news being shoved down our throats.

People have said that this is the worst economy since the Great Depression. This reminds me of the warrior David in 1 Samuel 17. The Philistine, Goliath, had tried over and over again to demoralize God's people. David said in 1 Samuel 17:32,33:

> "Don't worry about this Philistine," David told Saul. "I'll go fight him!"
>
> "Don't be ridiculous!" Saul replied. "There's no way you can fight this Philistine and possibly win! You're only a boy, and he's been a man of war since his youth."

We must confront the same negative voices today that say that we don't have the power and we don't have the strength to overcome the great odds against us. David's relationship with God was greater than the voices of intimidation. 1 Samuel 17:45-47 says:

> David replied to the Philistine, "You come to me with sword, spear, and javelin, but I come to you in the name of the LORD of Heaven's Armies—the God of the armies of Israel, whom you have defied. Today the LORD will conquer you, and I will kill you and cut off your head. And then I will give the dead bodies of your men to the birds and wild animals, and the whole world will know that there is a God in Israel! And everyone assembled here will know that the LORD rescues his people, but not with sword and spear. This is the LORD's battle, and he will give you to us!"

This is why many people fail to receive God's help and favor. They fail to understand that this battle is not natural; this is supernatural. David declared that the Lord will rescue us.

When God refreshed my thinking back in December of 2008, something changed on the inside of me. The oppression of negative reports was broken, and I began to think about expansion, vision, and outreach instead of conserving. I began to think about conquering and reaching more people than ever before. Instead of cutting back, I decided to expand, buy more airtime, and do everything that the enemy was trying to convince me not to do. This economy is an attack on the heart of the expander. God rewards a reacher.

The enemy is always trying to stop a dreamer's progress. God's people must always have a sense of mission and assignment. Faith goes into the realm of the unseen and materializes the blessing that you desire. Fear paralyzes the heart and causes negative things to happen. Lee Warren, in his report "The Negative Effect of Fear on The Mind," said that the most powerful forces known to man are not nuclear weapons or nature's awesome wonders, but the thoughts and ideas of the mind. The irony of thoughts or ideas is that no one has ever seen or handled them with physical senses, nor have the philosophers proven their existence. Yet everyone has personally conceived an idea and reflected on a thought in their mind. The mind always holds a thought or an idea. Warren goes on to report that various studies have shown the effect that thoughts have on the body and mind. Thoughts as ethereal as vapor have a profound effect. We hear stories of people dying in their sleep due to a frightening dream. People who are awake have actually been scared to death. So we can see that thoughts have a very powerful effect on the biochemistry of the physical body. Jesus said in Matthew 15:18-19, "But the words you speak come from the heart—that's what defiles you. For from the heart come evil thoughts, murder, adultery, all sexual immorality, theft, lying, and slander." These negative thoughts have a powerful effect on both mind and body.

That is the reason for this book—*Fearonomics*. In 2005, a book titled *Freakonomics* topped the New York Times bestsellers list. While that's a clever title, I realized that what I saw all around me could better be called *Fearonomics*—the fear that has been instilled in many people by news reports of gloom and doom. *Fearonomics* is intended to bring your "fight" back—to help you remember, or maybe realize for the first time, the goodness of God and the plan He has for you; to stomp out fear at first sight, because this force is designed to destroy your life. Don't be casual with fear; attack it with relentless resistance. God's plan is not just a spiritual plan but a natural plan as well. Stop allowing fear to rob you. You need to be like Rocky, the boxer. He had lost his fighting edge. Success had made him lazy. Only after he suffered a terrible loss in the ring did he *decide* to get his swagger back. *Fearonomics* is about getting your fighting edge back and keeping it, remembering who you are and Whose you are. So get your gloves on and get ready for the fight of your life. But always remember this: You've already won.

Enjoy the book!

1
LIONS AND TIGERS AND BEARS— OH, MY

―――――◆―――――

"This is my command—be strong and courageous! Do not be afraid or discouraged. For the Lord your God is with you wherever you go."

Joshua 1:9

Truly the yellow brick road is not as colorful as it used to be. Dorothy is not the only one who is afraid. An article in the April 2009 issue of *Vanity Fair* magazine asked if it is time to rethink the American dream. Over the course of the last two years, this world has changed its complexion. Even secular columnists are writing about our changing world in a way that almost depicts Bible times. The American dream is not what it used to be. People have watched college funds disintegrate and retirement funds shrink. Businesses and charities have been wiped out due to scam artists who have deceived the affluent and not-so-affluent. People have lost their homes. The two-children, two-car, one-spouse mentality is quickly disappearing from our view. So for the sake of foundation, let us define the term "fearonomics."

"Fearonomics" is an economy based on fear and self-preservation. God's plan in Scripture shows us the path of trusting in God and living a life of radical generosity. We see such scriptural figures as Isaac in the Old Testament, who in time of famine decided to make investments to sow seed. The Scripture records that God rewarded him with a hundredfold return in the same year. Isaiah 35:4 says, "Say to those with fearful hearts, 'Be strong, and do not fear, for your God is coming to destroy your enemies. He is coming to save you.'" Throughout the Word of God the phrase "fear not" is a very common theme.

Removing fear from your life is the first step to walking in victory. Fear immobilizes; faith empowers. In 1 Kings 17:13, "fear not" came before the widow could experience uncommon provision. Fear was her limiting factor. The prophet Elijah attacked the fear before he attacked the lack. Although the widow's need was great and she was ready to eat her last meal with her son, the prophet warned her to destroy fear or fear would destroy her. We need the words of faith to starve our doubts. It's not time to maintain; it's time to stretch forward. There is uncommon provision for the child of God who will not lose his or her hope. This is a great moment to be alive; it is a great moment to prove the power of God. The Church should arise with memorable power. This is our defining moment. The world is struggling to find hope, but the Church must remain hopeful. We must subdue our fears. Plant seeds against your natural instincts, and God will cause your provisions to rise to an overflowing level.

Years ago, I heard a story about two men flying in a single-engine airplane. The pilot, who was a Christian, leaned over to the unsaved businessman, said there were storms in the area, and suggested they join hands and pray. The businessman said, "My God—has it come to that?" Here was a gentleman who definitely looked at prayer as a last resort. The Bible teaches us to look to God first in everything;

He's never our last resort. In the midst of unrest and troubled times, God's people go to work. Our prayers prevail, and our God's power reigns supreme. Here is what *The Message Bible* says in 2 Corinthians 9:6-11:

> Remember: A stingy planter gets a stingy crop; a lavish planter gets a lavish crop. I want each of you to take plenty of time to think it over, and make up your own mind what you will give. That will protect you against sob stories and arm-twisting. God loves it when the giver delights in the giving.
>
> God can pour on the blessings in astonishing ways so that you're ready for anything and everything, more than just ready to do what needs to be done. As one psalmist puts it, He throws caution to the winds, giving to the needy in reckless abandon. His right-living, right-giving ways never run out, never wear out.

As we move deeper into this book, you will see that our economy is not based upon this world; God's economy is based upon Scripture. Giving to the needy with reckless abandon puts us in a position for the abundance of God. As you can see, the Scripture doesn't caution the believer to conserve but challenges the believer to give radically. There are numerous people in our church, Livingway Family Church, who are being blessed in tremendous ways by natural standards. This shouldn't be happening, but because they're plugged into God's economy, their businesses are prospering while others are failing. One man named Alex opened a business called 101 Fitness. Everyone said it was destined to fail, yet Alex was certain in his spirit that he had heard from God to start this business. After about two months, the windows of heaven opened. Alex volunteered to work with me on my own fitness, and when I first went it was easy to schedule a time. Now he's so busy it's difficult to get in to see him. The business is getting ready to double in size. The only thing Alex did that others didn't was pray and give, and the Lord honored his faith in a great way.

When everything looks scarce in the natural, that's when the ground is rich for expansion in the kingdom of God. According to second Corinthians, our most generous God, who gives the farmer the seed, is more than extravagant with you. He will give you a seed that you can give away. That seed will grow into your future wealth. You are free to be generous in every way, knowing that your generosity will produce a harvest.

In order for the widow in 1 Kings 17:10-16 to receive abundant provision in the midst of famine, she had to move past fear and act on the word of the prophet. In Joshua 1:9, the Lord said "fear not" before Joshua could reach his defining moment and become the next level leader for Israel. What does God want you to lead? For me personally, I had to go back to my visions and plans before economic disaster hit, look at what the Lord had told me to do, and realize His plan hadn't changed.

In Joshua 1, God spoke fresh courage and faith into Joshua's heart to convince him he could be an effective leader. As an "expander," you must always keep hope alive. It reminds me of the painting in a businessman's office of an old boat washed up on shore. Friends had told the businessman that the painting was depressing, but there was a caption underneath the painting that read, "The tide always comes back." The man said the painting served as a reminder that just because things are bad, don't despair—the tide always comes back. That's the faith of an expander. Things may be bad right now.

The world outlook may look grim, but the tide will move, life will change, and heaven will answer, so keep the faith.

You've heard me refer to the word "expander" several times. Let me explain. I believe there are three types of people: expanders, settlers, and nostalgics. In this time of financial challenge, you will find many settlers trying to keep what they have, content to maintain the status quo. In the end, the settlers end up losing out. The "conserve" mentality will eventually lose. I coach high school basketball for our Christian school, Livingway Christian School. The most critical time in the basketball game is not when we're losing; it's when we're ahead. The reason is that if we are tempted to settle, we lose our aggression, which gives the opposing team the advantage to get back in the game. Don't allow the same attitude to occur in life; keep playing as if you are always behind. This gives you the competitive edge.

The third type of people are the nostalgics. They're living in yesterday, thinking about how good the good old days were. As they say, the good old days weren't that good. I remember the other day, I wanted to find an old song we used to sing in church. When I looked it up and had the opportunity to listen to it, I realized that it wasn't as great as I thought it was. What happened to that song? It was the same song we used to enjoy, but at a different time. The song didn't change, but the times did. That's the danger of trying to hold on to what was; it was only good then, because it was designed for that time. Fresh manna for Israel illustrated the need for a fresh word from God. Every day requires a fresh response to God. Don't get nostalgic in spirit or you'll miss out on God's provision for today.

This has been compared to the dead horse theory. Dakota tribal wisdom says that when you discover you are riding a dead horse, the best strategy is to dismount. However, in churches we often try other strategies with dead horses. Here's the list: change riders, say things like "This is the way we've always ridden this horse," appoint a committee to study the horse, arrange a visit to other sites to see how they ride horses, change bylaws to specify that horses shall not die, harness several dead horses together for increased speed, declare that no horse is too dead to ride, provide additional funding to increase the horse's performance, and promote the dead horse to a supervisory position. It's funny, but it's also sad. If we do not change, we will stay in the pool of yesterday's provision. Remember, we're talking about "fear not."

Arthur Somers said, "Anxiety is a thin stream of fear trickling through the mind. If encouraged, it cuts a channel into which all other thoughts are drained." According to the *American Heritage Dictionary*, the definition for the word *fear* is "an emotion of alarm and agitation caused by the expectation or realization of danger." Agitation creates an expectation of disaster, so we could say that the root of fear is wrong vision.

In 2 Kings 6:16-17, it says, "'Don't be afraid!' Elisha told him. 'For there are more on our side than on theirs!' Then Elisha prayed, 'O LORD, open his eyes and let him see!' The LORD opened the young man's eyes, and when he looked up, he saw that the hillside around Elisha was filled with horses and chariots of fire." Here again we see the command "don't be afraid" leading the way into an open heaven. Fear is always an indication that we don't trust God fully. Let's remember we're on a mission to strangle even the scent of fear in our lives. Fear can blind us to God's incredible deliverance. Even though Elisha and his servant were surrounded by the enemy, heaven's assistance had been available the whole time.

In 2 Kings 6:8-10, the Bible says that before the Arameans could attack God's people, the prophet would tell the king where they were going and how they would mobilize. This made the opposing king very angry, but it meant that God's people were always informed about where the enemy was going and what he was about to do. As God's people, we should be in a similar position. We should be miles ahead of the enemy. We should know where to invest, when to invest, and what to invest. We must hear His words saying "do" when it's not convenient, and "act" when it's not in style. People who have lost sight of God's help are consumed with the loss of 401(k) plans and how the stimulus package will affect them. Let me remind you—there are more with us than there are against us. We are not surrounded by problems but by the hope and help of heaven.

In 1 Kings 17:13, the prophet said "fear not" to the widow. That "fear not" came before she could experience uncommon provision. For her it *was* provision; she had eaten her last meal. She had to move past fear, and trust the word of the prophet. Her trust unlocked her specific blessing. I believe that God has a specific blessing for every life. For the widow it was a material need, and maybe your need is a material need. Perhaps you have fallen behind and can't pay your bills, and you're under the load of a suffering economy. But God says "Move past your fear." You can't do anything when you are paralyzed by fear. You have to move past your fear to experience the provision of God.

In Joshua's case, he had to move past his fear to become the leader God wanted him to be. People were depending on him and his ministry, waiting on the word that God had shut up inside him. But he had to confront his personal fears. He had to overcome his fears that he wasn't suited to fill Moses' shoes or to fill that level of responsibility. When he confronted that intimidation, God moved him to the next level of leadership. Defeating his fears became Joshua's defining moment. He was able to lead Israel into fulfilling the incredible prophecy that God gave them. It would not be the last day that Joshua experienced conflict in his life There were still walled cities, and giants to defeat. There would be defeat at Ai and conflict among the people he was leading. But if he could move past his current intimidation, God had provided a season of divine leadership and divine breakthrough. God would give him a new day. Maybe that is your situation. Maybe your "fear not" has to do with your leadership—something God has put you in charge of, but you have not been willing to lead. Now is the time to move past your fear. Now is the time to confront your fear and receive the land that God has given you. You're the one to lead. You're the one God has called. Don't let fear serve as a barrier to keep you from the thing God has promised you.

As we have been studying from 1 Kings 6:16, for the prophet's servant, his "fear not" was that he had to stop looking at natural circumstances. He had to stop looking at the army that was surrounding them. Elisha prayed for the servant and said, "Lord, open his eyes. Open his eyes that he may see that there are more with us than there are against us." His "fear not" meant receiving a heavenly vision, looking with a different focus than he had been using before. So many people right now have their focus on the *need* and on what they hear from the media. Their focus is not on heaven or the opportunities that God has for them.

This is a season of opportunity. This is a season of blessing for the child of God. There is no cause for fear. This is the time for conquest. This is the time for celebration. This is a great time of opportunity.

The Scripture says we should sing, because we have this opportunity. God wants you to look through spiritual eyes, just as God gives eagles the ability to see through a storm. Heaven is rallying for you. Heaven has a plan. Malachi 3 says if we have a radical, generous heart, the heart of a giver, we can open the windows of heaven and not only see heaven's provision but receive heaven's provision. Heaven's provision will rain down in our life. That is an incredible thought. Before the servant could envision supernatural deliverance and see all that God had provided, he had to squelch his fear. Like him, we need to put our fear under our feet, conquer our fears and get a brand-new focus. God is still God, God is still good, and He is faithful. This book will help you redirect your focus, open your eyes, and show you that there is more *with* you—more possibility, more blessing, and more favor—than there is *against* you.

Zephaniah 1:6 says, "And I will destroy those who used to worship me but now no longer do. They no longer ask for the Lord's guidance or seek my blessings." If God said He would destroy those who used to worship Him, then this is a critical season of redirection. God can work in these difficult times to refocus our lives and our priorities back to Him. These are strong words, but many in our society have become fat and comfortable. We've believed we don't need God or His help, so these critical times of recession and economic downfall serve as a wake-up call to redirect our priorities. In this time, for many who forget to pray over a meal or forget to pray about God's guidance about their money, it's a whole new day. It's a brand new day, and people are praying like never before. It's like the bumper sticker says—"As long as there are tests there will be prayer in school." And we can say that about our lives—so long as there are tests, there will be prayer and people will be praying. God wants to be first in our lives. His guidance and blessing is imperative to our success. It is very clear that destruction is at hand for those who do not seek Him. But for those who turn and seek God's guidance, He makes incredible provision available to them.

Katherine Patterson said it this way: "To fear is one thing; to let fear grab you by the tail and swing you around is another." Some people, amidst all the negative reports, have let fear grab them and swing them around by the tail. It has been estimated that in the next four years there will be 10 million foreclosures. These words grip Americans and the rest of the world with fear, but the words of Jesus dispel fear.

Let's look at what Christ said in the Scriptures about our daily necessities and provision. Christ talked about money more than two thousand times in the four Gospels, more references than any other subject. As children of God we should be comforted concerning our finances as we hear the words Christ spoke concerning our finances.

Matthew 6:25-32 says,

> "That is why I tell you not to worry about everyday life—whether you have enough food and drink, or enough clothes to wear. Isn't life more than food, and your body more than clothing? Look at the birds. They don't plant or harvest or store food in barns, for your heavenly Father feeds them. And aren't you far more valuable to him than they are? Can all your worries add a single moment to your life?

> "And why worry about your clothing? Look at the lilies of the field and how they grow. They don't work or make their clothing, yet Solomon in all his glory was not dressed as beautifully as they are. And if God cares so wonderfully for wildflowers that are here today and thrown into the fire tomorrow, he will certainly

care for you. Why do you have so little faith?

"So don't worry about these things, saying, 'What will we eat? What will we drink? What will we wear?'These things dominate the thoughts of unbelievers, but your heavenly Father already knows all your needs."

Once again, here is an invitation to the child of God to eliminate anxiety. He said in Matthew 6:28, "And why worry about your clothing? Look at the lilies of the field and how they grow. They don't work or make their clothing, yet Solomon in all his glory was not dressed as beautifully as they are." In that day, kings traveled just to see the royalty and majesty of Solomon's Temple—all the grandeur and the wealth that it represented. Yet the Bible says that just as God clothed the lilies, which are clothed greater than Solomon's Temple, so will God clothe us and take care of us. God is good, and He is extravagant. As Scripture says, God lavishly blesses His people. We should not live off crumbs, or even look for the crumbs. When He has asked us to dine at the table of royalty, why would we settle for crumbs?

I love verse 32 as well, where Jesus says, "These things dominate the thoughts of unbelievers, but your heavenly Father already knows all your needs." In other words, don't allow your problems, worries, struggles, or bad news to dominate your thought life. You choose what you think about. Fill your mind and heart with the Word of the Lord. The Bible says, "Hath [God] said, and shall he not do it?" (Numbers 23:19 KJV). The Word of the Lord says, "Who hath believed our report? And to whom is the arm of the LORD revealed?" (Isaiah 53:1 KJV). The revelation of His hand is about understanding what is in His heart. In His heart is blessing, a desire to prosper us and give us a great future, according to Jeremiah 29:11. Jesus speaks sternly and vehemently against worry and anxiety and tells us to not allow these things to dominate our thoughts.

These are great times to prove God's power and prove the relevance of Scripture. The Word of the Lord says in Malachi 3:10 KJV, "prove me now herewith." God is inviting us to keep on giving and tithing and having a radical heart of generosity. He says, "I will open the windows of heaven for you and pour you out a blessing that there is not room for you to receive." *Prove Me, prove Me.* These are times to prove God. Expand your faith and your vision. Don't allow "fearonomics" to weigh your heart down and trouble your soul. Instead, begin to grow, expand, and build.

When the Lord spoke to us to build this ministry here in Brownsville, Texas, the city was-and still is-one of the poorest communities in America. Thank God we did not know that. We did not study demographics. We studied faith. We had to pay off a land debt of about $120,000 before we could start building, and the city was ready to tear down the community center where we had been meeting. We were coming down to the wire. As God began to move, He provided the finances from the most unlikely sources. We used a little rented run-down, single-wide office trailer, and I remember sitting there one day and heard a knock at the door. That's when the first sign of God's grace showed up. A dear lady came by and gave us a check for $25,000. It blew us away; the check was worth more than the office complex we were using. A few weeks later, my wife called me as I was coming home from a hospital visit. She told me another dear lady from the church wanted to give a donation. I was tired; it had been a long day, and I really did not want to go see this woman. But I decided to go anyway. When I met with her, I experienced another manifestation of God's grace—two checks that almost equaled the other $25,000 check.

Within the space of a few days, in what looked like an impossible situation, two unrelated parties had provided funds that canceled the land debt and allowed us to move ahead. When we moved into our sanctuary, it swallowed our little congregation. But before long we filled those chairs, and then we bought more chairs, and it looked like we would not fill those. But soon, we removed a wall—which looked like a move ahead of its time, but God filled that space. *I believe God will fill the container that you give Him.* If, in this hour, negative reports cause you to withdraw, no doubt you will see a movement backward instead of a movement forward. Keep pressing on, keep expanding in your faith, and keep expanding your vision.

As the prophet prayed for the servant—let his eyes be opened, let him see heaven's provision, let him see what already is—I am praying for you today that you will see what already is. Whether you see it or not, it's already there. Heaven is at your disposal, available to you, but the provision doesn't come until you see it. You must have *vision* in order for there to be *provision.* Remember what God said—*I will destroy those who do not worship Me and refuse to acknowledge My guidance and seek My blessing any longer.* Those are strong words; continue to seek God in the midst of it all.

For the next several chapters of this book I want to look at the words of Jesus, which, according to Romans 10:17, instill faith and drive out the fear. When I heard from God in the early part of December 2008, He thundered inside of me: It's time to get your focus back and remember who you are, because in the midst of all the bad news it is easy to forget who you are and the promise you have with Me.

Our covenant with God is the number one reason not to fear. We are people of covenant. We have a binding agreement with

God that keeps us regardless of what happens on this planet. God's economy is higher than man's. We do not deny reality, but instead of misplacing our faith, we must refocus our faith. One of the greatest truths in Scripture for the people of God is that we have an incredible covenant with God that governs our lives. That's hard for us to grasp as Westerners. If we were from the Middle East it would be easier for us to understand, because people from that area are people of covenants. But according to Ephesians 2:12, we are strangers to the covenants of promise. Covenant terms are strange to us, according to the Word of God. It's hard for us to think in terms of covenant because we live in a promise-breaker society. It's difficult for us to think as promise keepers. But our God is a promise keeper, and He invites us to be promise keepers as well. The Scripture identifies us as "children of promise."

So let's refocus on the power of God's covenant. Let your faith grow, and your doubts cease. Remember when you were a child? I do. I had a lot of fears. As a child, I had an unreasonable fear of death. Every time I was sick or injured or something bad happened, I would ask my parents, "Am I going to die? Am I going to die?" That was constantly coming out of my mouth. I remember hearing, "No, son, you are not going to die. This is not 'unto death.' Daddy's with you, Mommy's with you. You are going to be all right."

Later in life, I was able to comfort my own children, but my wife is the better comforter. I am not very good with blood and stuff like that. My wife is definitely the mercy manifestation, in our marriage, our relationship, and our family. But nevertheless, I am able to pass comfort on to my children, letting them hear the words of Dad and the words of Mom saying, "I am with you"—that drives the fear away. The first step to us overcoming fear in our lives is to understand that the Father is with us. He gave us His promises. We have a covenant with the Father that the Father will not break, irrevocable and irreversible. The covenant is keeping us, when we are awake, when we are asleep, when we are in trouble, when we are in danger, when we are in tough times, and when we are in prosperous times. The covenant is keeping us through all of those times and seasons.

One of the areas of Scripture that we tend to glaze over is found in Luke 22, where Jesus sits down with His disciples at the last Passover meal. His powerful words are all about covenant. Jesus came to establish a new covenant—to fulfill what was spoken in the old covenant and then solidify it in the new covenant by His blood. Luke 22:20 says, "After supper He took another cup of wine and said 'This cup is the new covenant between God and his people— an agreement confirmed with my blood which is poured out as a sacrifice for you.'" Jesus said the cup represents the new covenant. Think of it—you are drinking into this covenant. Your life is mingled and is unified with the words Jesus spoke over His disciples. You have become the covenant of God. Christ went on to say that this agreement was confirmed with His blood. This was before He went to Calvary and shed His blood, but He was giving His disciples a prophetic insight that the cup would be a symbol of the new covenant. On the cross, He validated these claims by the shedding of blood.

The shedding of Jesus' blood signifies the strongest form of covenant. This is not ordinary blood. This is the blood of the precious Lamb of God. John said, "Behold the Lamb of God which taketh away the sin of the world" (John 1:19 KJV). Jesus took away the sting of death in His blood, in His death, burial, and resurrection. He removed our limitations and liabilities. He absorbed every inferior element of our life with His covenant blood. He infused into you and me the divine ability of almighty God. Why should I be afraid? Why should I fear, when the Lord is so overwhelmingly on my side? Why should *you* fear? God is on your side, and the covenant is keeping you.

Through Christ, God invited us into covenant. To get a deeper understanding of covenant, we need to go back to the Old Testament. An excellent example of covenant is the agreement that God made with Abraham, "the father of faith." No one else in Scripture receives such an accolade. Look to Abraham if you want to understand faith. Hebrews 11:6 KJV says, "Without faith it is impossible to please [God]...he that cometh to God must believe that he is and that he is a rewarder of those who diligently seek him." We want to please God and bring Him honor, so we must be a people of faith.

Genesis 15 explains covenant. God promised Abram that He would bless him exceedingly. He told him to look up into the sky and count the stars—that was how many descendents he would have. Abram believed the Lord, and God called him righteous because of his faith. Abram replied to the Lord, "How can I be sure I will actually possess it?" (Genesis 15:8). Abram was asking for a sign, something that would seal the deal and confirm the oath that God had promised—that his seed would be great upon the earth. Abram was in his 70s at this time. His wife was around the same age and had been barren. This was an impossible situation, which also shows us the heart and mind of God. God speaks into our impossibilities and declares that *it shall be.* If it was possible and attainable, we would not need God's help or His miraculous provision.

Today, God is speaking us to step out, plant a seed, or start a new business, when everything in the natural is contrary to that.

Your emotions are screaming at you, *Don't do it! Don't step out! Wait until another time or place! Wait until it gets better!* These are the days of proving God, when God honors those who step out in faith and step out on the water. God will support you supernaturally as you step out in faith.

Abram was asking God how he could have "many descendants." So God took it to the next level. In the next verses, from verse 9 through 17, a covenant ceremony was set up. There were animals, and bloodshed. The blood ran, and Abram stood in the midst of the blood. Genesis 15:17-18 says, "After the sun went down and the darkness fell, Abram saw a smoking firepot and flaming torch pass between the halves of the carcasses. So the LORD made a covenant with Abram that day." God made a covenant with Abram, a covenant set in blood. In the midst of the blood, God declared, "I have given this land to your descendants all the way from the border of Egypt to the great Euphrates River" (Genesis 15:18 NLT). The covenant was declared in blood and established by blood.

That is why Christ spoke those powerful words in the book of Luke. He took the cup and said, let this represent the new covenant. Let this represent a new beginning and it will be ratified by My blood. When My blood is shed, this covenant will be consummated. Hence the declaration on the cross: It is finished. Jesus signed the final document, declaring that the blood was shed. God declared that the Holy of Holies is now open. We can come into His presence; fellowship, partake, live, dwell, walk in the precious glory of almighty God. This was an incredible breakthrough for the people of God.

Genesis 15:14 says, "I will punish the nations that enslave them and in the end they will come again with great wealth." The Lord made it clear that just because you are a child of God does not mean you are exempt from problems. He made it clear that your enemies will come against you, but when they come against you they will be enslaved. In the same manner, you will come away with great wealth. God is speaking to us to realign ourselves with the covenant promise of God in this day and in this hour. We need to realize that God is still speaking to us and that the covenant is alive through the blood of Jesus. He says that we are going to come away with great wealth. No doubt we are in a great challenge right now, and we are facing problems in our country and our financial arena. But our hope is not this world or material things. Remember what Christ said in Matthew 6. Don't allow material things to dominate your mind.

Vanity Fair published an article about the thousands of people who had lost money in Bernie Madoff's Ponzi scheme. Some people lost life savings of $400,000 and others $5 million, while whole charities were wiped out. Many of these people were in great despair. The social events where they gathered were like a funeral, because of depression and discouragement over the loss of funds. But children of God should understand that money is not where our joy comes from. Our lives do not consist of the things that we possess. Our joy comes from the Lord, a deeper source. We have a covenant with God that says that in the end we are going to come away with great wealth.

Right now, as you are reading this book, your life may be challenging. You may feel as if your career is in the pits. Remember Joseph? He was in an actual pit! His story is in Genesis 37 and 38. But Joseph did not stay in the pit, and I have great news for you. Although you might feel as if your life is in a pit, you do not have to stay there. God said, you're going to come away with more than you went in with. You're coming away with great wealth. It is in the covenant. It was promised in the covenant.

Genesis 17:1 says, "When Abram was ninety-nine years old, the LORD appeared to him and said, 'I am El Shaddai—"God Almighty." Serve me faithfully and live a blameless life.'" Every promise is conditional—there is something for us to do. At times we want to place the responsibility on God to be faithful. You don't have to worry; that is His character. He will be faithful. Everything He promised you, He will do. But sometimes we lack the integrity and the character. God says that you need to serve Him faithfully and live a blameless life. That is not the same as a perfect life. A blameless life is a life pursuing God, His power, His approval, and His grace in our lives. The Lord appeared and declared, "I am El Shaddai, I am the almighty God." The name *El Shaddai* means "I am more than enough. I am more than enough for you." God is our "more than enough." In Genesis 17:2-6, He says,

> "I will make a covenant with you, by which I will guarantee to give you countless descendents."
>
> At this, Abram fell face down on the ground. Then God said to him, "This is my covenant with you: I will make you the father of a multitude of nations! What's more, I am changing your name. It will no longer be Abram. Instead, you will be called Abraham, for you will be the father of many nations. I will make you extremely fruitful. Your descendents will become many nations and kings will be among them!"

Let's look at this series of promises very closely. First of all, in verse 2 God said, "I will make a covenant with you by which I will guarantee to give you countless descendents." The covenant is your guarantee. Look at how Abraham received the word. Our hearts need to look like Abraham's in order to receive God's blessings. I have heard the Word of God for years and have had great things spoken over my life. But we are not always in the right place to receive the right word. It could be the right word at the wrong place and time in our lives. Our hearts have to be ready for it. The promise is incredible, but how we receive it determines the full impact that the promise will have in our lives.

When he received knowledge and further validation of God's covenant, Abram fell down on the ground. He literally fell down and worshiped God. Our response to God is so critical. We could just take this word and say, "Well, I have heard that before" or "That's just another sermon" or "You don't know my problem" or "You don't know the degree—they have taken everything. They're are coming to take my car today, my house is next in line for foreclosure, I have been laid off, and there are a hundred other applicants ahead of me." You can focus right there all day long, but all you're doing is digging a deeper grave. Through worship, you can get your heart in the right place to receive from God. Worship is saying to God, "I believe in You. I validate Your Word for my life. I accept that Word. I become that Word." This is what Abraham did when he fell on his face and began to worship God. He was saying, "I am becoming the Word that God is speaking over me."

God began to tell Abraham about multitudes of blessing. In verse 5, He said, "What's more, I am changing your name from Abram to Abraham." That is significant. To go from a father of *altitude* (high faith) to a father of *multitude* is a big switch. I love the teaching that says because Abraham was able to *see* it—the father of altitude—he was able to *become* it—the father of multitude.

It was once commonplace for a name change to accompany covenant agreements. When a covenant began between two parties, there was typically a name change. If you were from the Middle

East, you would quickly understand that this was now Abraham's covenant name. It represented a new identity. Before, there was no covenant, but after, there is a covenant with someone who is superior and who has the power to bless His covenant partner. These are not false hopes or false dreams. These are promises with strength and power.

In verse 6, God says, "I will make you extremely fruitful. Your descendants will become many nations, and kings will be among them!" I believe that God will make your life fruitful. I believe God wants your business, your home life, and your investments to grow. He wants fruit to come out of dry places, out of a place of famine. God will increase your life and give you greater abundance than you have ever had before.

2

A GENERATIONAL COVENANT

The covenant is generational. In Genesis 28, Jacob wrestled with God and then obeyed. We can go back and we see Isaac in Genesis 26, and how God spoke to him. Remember the sequence: Abraham, Isaac and Jacob. The covenant that was alive in Abraham was alive in his seed. This is why we see, all the way down through David and to Christ and to us, that the covenant is still alive today. The covenant didn't cease to exist. God did not unplug it somewhere along the way. We are still plugged into the benefits and the blessings that the Word promised we would have.

God spoke to Isaac in Genesis 26:2-5, "The Lord appeared to Isaac and said 'Do not go down to Egypt, but do as I tell you. Live here as a foreigner in this land, and I will be with you and bless you. I hereby confirm that I will give all these lands to you and your descendants, just as I solemnly promised Abraham, your father. I will cause your descendents to become as numerous as the stars of the sky and I will give them all these lands. And through your descendents all the nations of the earth will be blessed. I will do this because Abraham listened to me and obeyed all my requirements, commands, decrees and instructions.'" Isaac received a similar prophecy as his father. God was very direct in verse 5, saying that this was not because Isaac was so great; it was because of his father. It was because of the covenant. It was not by his own good works or by his own talent. "I will do this because Abraham listened to me and obeyed."

We are in a similar position today. God is saying to us, "I am going to bless you because it's My covenant. Maybe you have strayed away and lost focus, but guess what? I am going to bless you anyway. I love you, and I am going to bless you. I am going to remind you of the covenant over your life." So Isaac, armed with this knowledge, continued in God's will. The Word tells us in Genesis 26:12-13, "When Isaac planted his crops that year, he harvested a hundred times more grain than he planted, for the LORD blessed him. He became a very rich man and his wealth continued to grow." Who blessed him? The Lord blessed him. For those who disagree with prosperity and don't think that God want us to be blessed, remember it is God who is doing the blessing. He chose to bless and He wants us to prosper, so let's not fight against God in our thinking. Rather, we need to put ourselves in a position to receive His goodness and His favor.

Isaac became a very rich man, and his wealth continued to grow. He acquired so many flocks of sheep and goats, herds of cattle, and servants that the Philistines became jealous of him. If you give God the glory, you can become the envy of this world, too.

Genesis 26:15-16 says, "So the Philistines filled up all of Isaac's wells with dirt. These were the wells that had been dug by the servants of his father, Abraham. Finally Abimelech ordered Isaac to leave the country. 'Go somewhere else' he said, 'for you have become too powerful for us.'" This is an interesting phrase to understand. The Philistines are the chronic enemy of the people of God. They are always the enemy of advancement, representing harassment.

Many of you who have trusted God and have seen God's blessing have experienced the Philistines coming to fill your wells back up with mud. It's as if they are throwing dirt on your vision, trying to bury your dreams under the dirt of mediocrity. There are those who are jealous of your progress, and so is the enemy. If you are facing resistance, that's a great sign. It means you're moving in the right direction. Keep moving. Keep stretching.

Isaac could have stopped right there, but the Bible tells us that he re-dug the wells of his father, Abraham. That refers to wise planning and setting goals. So many people have just pulled back the forces, folded up the tents, packed up the wagons, and are heading home. Don't pack up the wagons and retreat; re-dig the wells and create a new opportunity. When Isaac re-dug the wells, he was saying, "I'm preparing for water flow, I am preparing for increase. This land will be fruitful. This land will be blessed by God."

Why would Isaac do that? Because he understood that he was a man of covenant. When the Lord appeared to him, God said, "I am the God of your father, Abraham' he said. 'Do not be afraid, for I am with you and will bless you. I will multiply your descendants, and they will become a great nation. I will do this because of My promise to Abraham, my servant." (Genesis 26:24). Once again God reminded Isaac of the nature and origin of the blessing on his life. We must keep that central in everything we do. Genesis 26:25 says, "Then Isaac built an altar there and worshipped the LORD. He set up his camp at that place, and his servants dug another well." That's great advice for those who are looking for hope and direction today! Build an altar and worship God. It doesn't matter what the Philistines try to do to stop you—how much dirt they throw in your well or how they try to stop your forward progress. Build an altar and worship God. Give God His rightful place.

Remember when God spoke His awesome, incredible plan and purpose for Abraham's life in Genesis 17? His initial reaction was not "I am Abraham! Look at me! I'm great! Look what I've done!" His initial reaction was to fall on his face and acknowledge the goodness of God. That perpetuates the blessing of God in our lives; it causes the blessings to keep coming and coming.

We need to set up camp where God tells us. Pitch your tent and build your life on the Word of God, because God has a divine locator for blessing in your life: X marks the spot. He will bless where He speaks and what He speaks. Just like Isaac's servants dug another well, we can dig a new well. God will tell us where to dig – this is an area of new expansion, because this is where God's Word is.

I believe God is showing many of you how you can dig another well and provide for the next level of blessing in your life. Remember that this covenant is generational. We come right along in line after Abraham, Isaac, and Jacob. Genesis 28 speaks of a season of wrestling with God, as many of you have wrestled late into the night over what you're going to do, where your next paycheck is going to come from, and how you are going to pay that next credit card payment. You may have wrestled in the midnight hour, but eventually God is going to win.

Genesis 28:20-21 says, "Then Jacob made this vow: if God will indeed be with me and protect me on this journey, and if he will provide me with food and clothing and, if I return safely to my father's home, then the Lord will certainly be my God.'" Jacob is acknowledging that God is his provision. Genesis 28:22 continues, "And this memorial pillar I have set up will become a place of worshipping God and I will present to God a tenth of everything that He gives me." In every generation where there is a revelation of covenant, that generation is quick to honor God with a financial offering. To get along well, have a good journey, and have food and clothing for the journey is one of the purest definitions of Hebrew prosperity.

One of the words that keeps coming up as we study covenant is the word *remember*: remember the Lord, remember the terms of the covenant, remember the God who gave the promise to you. We have to constantly be reminded, and remind ourselves, that God is with us. He will provide food and clothing for this journey, and He will be our God. Then what flows out of your worship is the giving not only of yourself, but also of material things to God. Jacob said, "I will present to God a tenth of everything he gives me." That becomes part of our worship. If you allow tough financial times to keep you from giving, that is exactly what the enemy will use to shut you down.

What ultimately happens to Jacob? Genesis 30:43 says, "As a result, Jacob became very wealthy, with large flocks of sheep and goats, male and female servants, and many camels and donkeys." God also gave Jacob tremendous wisdom. Remember the story of how he worked and labored for Laban? (Genesis 30:25-43). He asked Laban to give him all the spotted and speckled animals of the herd. Jacob had a revelation, and he peeled some branches and put them in the watering trough so the herds could see the image of the spotted and the speckled. They bred according to the image before them—in this case, the peeled branches that Jacob put in the trough. This is a clear example of the power of vision: what you look at long enough, you will become. You will produce what you see in your vision. If you continue to see the lack and problems around you, then that is all you will have. You allow your vision to seal your fate.

But vision can be fueled from the inside by the Word of God. That vision is the prophet for your future and will transform your life. Jacob had a revelation of that, and he walked in it mightily. It is time for you to break into an arena where nothing is outside of your hand. Squelch your fears, squelch your worries, and begin to trust God on a whole new level. Charles Spurgeon made the comment, "It has been said that our anxiety does not empty tomorrow of its sorrow. It only empties today of its strength." Perhaps you have allowed negative reports to drain you of your strength today. Take back your position in God and realize you have a covenant with Him. Because of this covenant, you need not fear.

Psalm 27:1 KJV says, "The LORD is my light and my salvation, whom shall I fear? The LORD is the strength of my life; of whom shall I be afraid?" When we look to the Lord, fear is removed from our lives. When we keep God central, we allow faith to rule supreme in our hearts. We have a covenant with God. We are a people of hope and promise. You need a change in your heart - a paradigm shift - the way you see life has to change.

Several years ago we were called out to minister to a man who was very troubled. He was oppressed of devils or something, and he began to speak out and mock and laugh at us. I remember for a second feeling intimidated, but then somewhere in the process, something shifted in my soul and I realized that he was more afraid of us than we were of him. Then with authority, I began to confront the situation from that point on and move to a position where we could help and deliver the poor man.

That is what needs to happen regarding your finances. The Spirit of the Lord needs to shoot through you like electricity and remind you that there are more with you than there are against you. When you realize this, you can move forward with greater confidence, knowing that you are a person of covenant and that the covenant is backing you up.

In 1 Samuel 22, we find the story of David fleeing from Saul. David had a purpose assigned to his life. He had already been promised the throne. He had been promised great things. But there were circumstances opposing his deliverance and his coming to greatness. As he fought his obstacles, he sought refuge in the house of God. Ahimelech, the priest at that time, consulted the Lord for him and gave him food and provision. At the end of the visit, Ahimelech did something interesting. He reached back in the storeroom, and pulled out the very same sword David had used to slay Goliath. All of a sudden, David's fears and intimidations melted, because somebody had reminded him that God had done great things in his past and that same God was still with him.

The Lord is saying this to you again today, reminding you of your past victories. God has set a precedent of providing and taking care of you. You have been through this before. You've slain your Goliath. You have stood alone with God before, and God has upheld you and been with you. God is reminding you again, as you seek sanctuary in the house of God, "Here is the sword. Rely on the Word. The Word of the Lord is the sword of the Lord. Trust in the Word. Speak the Word."

In Ephesians 6, the apostle Paul teaches us to take the sword of the Spirit, the Word of God, to launch an offensive against the enemy. The word that is used there is *wield*, which means to "use with skill." Paul says: take the Word of God on purpose and skillfully use it and speak it. Speak your covenant with authority and power. Try these scriptures to build your faith (emphasis mine):

- Use this scripture to remember where wealth comes from: *And you shall remember the LORD your God, for it is **He who gives you power to get wealth**, that He may establish His covenant which He swore to your fathers, as it is this day.* Deuteronomy 8:18 NKJV

- Use this scripture to help with carrying out your financial plans: *Therefore, since we are surrounded by such a great cloud of witnesses, let us throw off everything that hinders and the sin that so easily entangles, and let us **run with perseverance the race marked out for us**.* Hebrews 12:1 NIV

- Use this scripture to deal with your debt: *Jesus answered and said unto them, Verily I say unto you, If ye have faith, and doubt not, ye shall not only do this which is done to the fig tree, but also if ye shall say unto this mountain, **Be thou removed, and be thou cast into the sea**; it shall be done.* Matthew 21:21 KJV

- Use this scripture to keep perspective on what's important: *But seek ye **first** the kingdom of God, and his righteousness; and **all these things shall be added** unto you.* Matthew 6:33 KJV

- Use this scripture to understand God's desire to bless you abundantly: *Whereby are given unto us **exceeding great and precious promises**: that by these ye might be partakers of the divine nature, having escaped the corruption that is in the world through lust.* 2 Peter 1:4 KJV

- Use this scripture to build your expectation of blessings after you tithe or give offerings: *Give, and it will be given to you.* **A good measure, pressed down, shaken together and running over, will be poured into your lap.** *For with the measure you use, it will be measured to you.* Luke 6:38 NIV

In Hebrews 8:6, Christ said that we now have a better covenant—a new covenant—that is established on better promises. This covenant is still in force today. It has increased in strength and power, and we benefit from the strength of a covenant that was in place even before we were born. When we are born again through the power of salvation, through the power of receiving Christ's forgiveness, we are born into the covenant. This is an incredible union, an incredible institution that has been set up for our benefit and for our blessing. As we live faithfully before God, our lives are invigorated and stimulated. Our lives are stimulated by the promises God has spoken in and around and through and over our lives. The New Testament identifies this as a better covenant. You talk about a stimulus package!

Ephesians 2:11-12 says, "Don't forget that you Gentiles used to be outsiders. You were called 'uncircumcised heathens' by the Jews, who were proud of their circumcision, even though it affected only their bodies and not their hearts. In those days you were living apart from Christ. You were excluded from citizenship among the people of Israel, and you did not know the covenant promises God had made to them. You lived in this world without God and without hope." People without a covenant live in darkness. They are living without hope. Where there is no covenant, there is no expectation of victory. Hope is our anchor. We have to depend on it; we have to lean upon the hope we have been given in Christ as a reality of the covenant.

In the New King James Version, verse 12 says, "You were ...aliens from the commonwealth of Israel." The covenant represents a commonwealth. Those who are in covenant share the same opportunity for blessing in the kingdom of God. We all share the same opportunity for provision and prosperity, yet some of us fail to see the provision. We fail to activate our faith to cause that provision to happen in our lives. Yet we all have the same opportunity. Thank God there is a commonwealth, a common strength. You don't have to live your days apart from Christ. Live your life in His citizenship, included in the promises that we have through Christ Jesus. We are a people of hope.

We can walk in the same steps of faith that Abraham did and receive the same covenant blessings, today, this month, this year. You have to follow the steps of faith. What are the steps?

VISION

Abraham caught the vision that God had for his life. God painted an awesome vision when He said that his seed was going to be like the stars of the sky. Abraham could easily lift his head and see the great promises of God. God gives you and me a visual example, too. Our visual is the Word of God. Second Peter 1:4 calls them "great and precious promises." You have to see what God sees in you.

The covenant declarations from Deuteronomy 28:1-14 NIV are listed below. You ought to familiarize yourself with these promises, so you know what belongs to you, so you can declare them and see yourself in them and speak them and become them. These are things God spoke to Abraham that are fulfilled in Christ, through Christ's blood.

If you fully obey the LORD your God and carefully follow all his commands I give you today, the LORD your God will set you high above all the nations on earth. All these blessings will come on you and accompany you if you obey the LORD your God: You will be blessed in the city and blessed in the country. The fruit of your womb will be blessed, and the crops of your land and the young of your livestock—the calves of your herds and the lambs of your flocks. Your basket and your kneading trough will be blessed. You will be blessed when you come in and blessed when you go out. The LORD will grant that the enemies who rise up against you will be defeated before you. They will come at you from one direction but flee from you in seven. The LORD will send a blessing on your barns and on everything you put your hand to. The LORD your God will bless you in the land he is giving you. The LORD will establish you as his holy people, as he promised you on oath, if you keep the commands of the LORD your God and walk in his ways. Then all the peoples on earth will see that you are called by the name of the LORD, and they will fear you. The LORD will grant you abundant prosperity—in the fruit of your womb, the young of your livestock and the crops of your ground—in the land he swore to your ancestors to give you. The LORD will open the heavens, the storehouse of his bounty, to send rain on your land in season and to bless all the work of your hands. You will lend to many nations but will borrow from none. The LORD will make you the head, not the tail. If you pay attention to the commands of the LORD your God that I give you this day and carefully follow them, you will always be at the top, never at the bottom. Do not turn aside from any of the commands I give you today, to the right or to the left, following other gods and serving them.

SPEAK THE VISION

The second thing to do is speak these precious promises. Not only did Abraham see it—step number one—but he also said it: "I will be a father of many nations. My name is no longer Abram but Abraham." We are to speak the Word throughout the day. Any time we're tempted to think negative thoughts, God's Word needs to be right there to counteract them.

Here's an example of how you can speak the precious promises from Deuteronomy 28:

I thank You, Lord, that because I am obedient to Your Word, You have promised that You will bless me abundantly. I am blessed wherever I go. My children are blessed, and my business is blessed. My family and I always have enough to eat and enough money in our checking and savings accounts. I am blessed going in and blessed going out. Even if people try to hurt me or my family, they will be defeated. The work that I do is blessed, and the seeds that I plant will reap an abundant harvest. I lend to many nations and borrow from none; debt has no place in my life. Because I am obedient, I am the head and not the tail, above and not beneath. God has blessed me indeed!

BEING THE VISION

When you move from seeing to saying and declaring your vision with authority, then you will come into that third level of *being* it. The covenant becomes your identity. In other words, you see yourself as no other way: *I refuse to settle for second best. I am blessed. I prosper, because I know prosperity is the will of my Father. Whatever is opposing me is not from Him but is the enemy. Therefore, since God is with me, no one can be against me!*

Galatians 3:29 says, "now that you belong to Christ, you are the true children of Abraham." Some would teach in doctrines of dispensationalism that this promise only includes the literal blood children of Abraham. But Galatians 3:29 says that because of the blood of Jesus, we have become children of Abraham as well, if we belong to Christ. I hope you can see the covenant link all the way from the Old Testament in Genesis 15 to Galatians 3, saying that if you are in relationship with Christ, you are in relationship with the covenant.

Christ spoke about this at the last Passover meal with His disciples. As He lifted the cup, He said this is a new covenant and the new covenant is a reality through His blood. (Luke 22:20.) This is not fictional; this is reality. You have entered into a very prosperous family, the family of God. You have the covenant rights of an heir.

God spoke to Abraham in Deuteronomy 28, as a part of this Abrahamic covenant or blessing. Deuteronomy 28:1 says, "If you fully obey the LORD your God and carefully follow all his commands I give you today, the LORD your God will set you high above all the nations on earth. All these blessings will come on you and accompany you if you obey the LORD your God." The covenant is conditional upon our obedience. First things first: God wants our love. He wants relationship with us. He wants to be central in our lives. In Matthew 6:33 KJV He said, "But seek ye first the kingdom of God, and his righteousness; and all these things shall be added unto you." Loving Him should be our primary motive, and then all the material things will follow.

The blessings that God promised His people are the blessings you can claim in Christ. This is one of the greatest things God is doing through this time of financial crisis. I believe God is elevating the people of God to a brand-new level. This is the time for God's people to emerge the victor. This is the time for God's people to take center stage on the world scene, and all the nations will see that we are a people claimed by God—and they will stand in awe.

It would be incredible for CNN and Fox News to invite people of God on their interview programs and let them talk about how even in a struggling economy, people are prospering and good things are happening. All around them, factories and plants are closing and people are losing their jobs, yet there is this group of people. Could God make it that obvious? Could there be such a contrast between us and the world that it is that evident in this hour? I believe with all my heart that God is doing this. What the enemy has meant for evil, God will turn it around for good. God is turning a very ugly situation into a beautiful opportunity for the people of God.

One particular gentleman at the McAllen campus of Livingway Family Church has been a manager over a large factory. God has placed him in a very influential role. This particular factory has been on the chopping block. The region that we live in is known as one of the poorest regions in the United States. If any one of these factories was going to close down, it was going to be his factory. But in the end, the Japanese consolidated all the other factories into this central factory in the Rio Grande Valley, giving this gentleman more responsibility and putting him in a stronger position with more influence than he had before. What looked like impending defeat became a promotion for the child of God.

Everyone who is reading this can receive the spirit of promotion through this book. It's time to increase; God will not let you suffer harm. The psalmist David declared in Psalm 37:25 KJV, "I have not seen the righteous forsaken, nor His seed begging bread." God has a plan for the righteous. God has always supplied for those who love

Him. He is faithful. As the psalmist reflects that God has been his continual supplier, he is reminding himself and us that it's not God's will for us to beg. God did not call us to be beggars. He called us to prosper and be examples in the earth.

David's assurance of the Lord's leadership and His provision shows in Psalm 23, as David said, "The LORD is my shepherd; I shall not want" (KJV). The actual shepherd is responsible for every need of his flock, from their safety, to their food and drink, to their shelter. David understood that his food, his well-being, his protection, and his future are held in the hands of the Shepherd. And He is a good shepherd, so He is keenly aware of the needs of His people and He will provide. That is what God is doing today for those who trust Him and believe—just as with this gentleman over at the factory. When it looked as if all was lost, God turned the situation around and made it even better than before. We serve an awesome God.

Luke 13:10-16 says:

> One Sabbath day as Jesus was teaching in a synagogue, he saw a woman who had been crippled by an evil spirit. She had been bent double for eighteen years and was unable to stand up straight. When Jesus saw her, he called her over and said, "Dear woman, you are healed of your sickness!" Then he touched her, and instantly she could stand straight. How she praised God!
>
> But the leader in charge of the synagogue was indignant that Jesus had healed her on the Sabbath day. "There are six days of the week for working," he said to the crowd. "Come on those days to be healed, not on the Sabbath."
>
> But the Lord replied, "You hypocrites! Each of you works on the Sabbath day! Don't you untie your ox or your donkey from its stall on the Sabbath and lead it out for water? This dear woman,

a daughter of Abraham, has been held in bondage by Satan for eighteen years. Isn't it right that she be released, even on the Sabbath?"

This Scripture reveals many truths. One of them, according to the old Talmudic law, is one that the Pharisees did not even truly understand. They misquoted the essence of the Law. Jesus challenged them, pointing out that they would care for an ox or a donkey, to give them water on the Sabbath. Is it not right that this child of God—Jesus calls her a daughter of Abraham—should be healed on the Sabbath day? Jesus immediately connects her need with the covenant she had with God. Because of that covenant, there was no obstacle to her being healed.

Jesus reminds the Pharisees of the covenant. This woman is a daughter of Abraham, and as a daughter of Abraham she had the right to be healed on that day or any other day. It was right and fitting to God. I love the phrasing of verse 16 in the NLT. It says, "Isn't it right that she be released, even on the Sabbath?" In other words, the word "right" implies that there is authority. There is an authority, a right, and a precedent for this woman to be healed on this particular day.

A lot of people are bent over from financial strain or anxiety or some stress in their lives. Circumstances have laid them low. Some people have been embarrassed or humbled because of work-related situations or jobs or money that they lost. But Christ stands you up straight, gives you back your dignity, and restores you to your place in the world. If you know that you are a covenant child of God, you can stand up in the face of negative situations. In this woman's case, it was the religious right that tried to tell her how she could be healed, when she could be healed, and who could heal her, but the covenant of God circumvented all the natural limitations and fleshly criticisms. The covenant of God is above that. Because she is a daughter of Abraham through Christ, it is right and fitting for her to be healed.

You are a child of the Most High God, who has every right to access healing and the promises of God for prosperity and blessings in your life. Don't let anybody tell you that you can't have it. Don't let anybody deny you of it. Believe it with all your heart. It's up to you to believe it, just like the man in Mark 9:24 who said, "I do believe, but help me overcome my unbelief!" Pray that God will modify any area of your life where doubt and fear reside. Rise in faith. Don't allow fear to have a place in your life any longer.

Let's look at what the Word of God says in Psalm 91. The psalmist had a revelation of God's protection over his life. Sing a new song today—a song of trust, a song of faith, a new song of stability in the Lord. Psalm 91:1,2 says, "Those who live in the shelter of the Most High will find rest in the shadow of the Almighty. This I declare about the LORD: He alone is my refuge, my place of safety; he is my God, and I trust him." The psalmist had a revelation of living under the shelter of the Lord: God would take him under His wings and protect him from the traps that terrorize people.

Psalm 91:5 says, "Do not be afraid of the terrors of the night, nor the arrow that flies in the day." I feel like adding in "nor the stock market report, nor the economic outlook, nor the mortgage crisis." We could talk at length about the negative things that surround us, but our faith in the Lord must be strong. Psalm 91:9-12 says, "If you make the LORD your refuge, if you make the Most High your shelter, no evil will conquer you, no plague will come near your home. For he will order his angels to protect you wherever you go. They will hold you up with their hands so you won't even hurt your foot on a stone."

It's time to rejoice and be exceedingly glad, children of God, that we have a covenant of protection over our lives. Your job: don't fear! Your job is to declare that the Lord is your refuge, your place of safety. This is a declaration in the face of adversity. This is a declaration in the face of very negative circumstances. It is a declaration of faith to say that the Lord is my God and I trust in Him. You have to make that declaration even when it feels difficult to trust the Lord. In the latter part of this chapter, Psalm 91:14 says:

> The LORD says, "I will rescue those who love me.
>   I will protect those who trust in my name.
> When they call on me, I will answer;
>   I will be with them in trouble.
>   I will rescue and honor them.
> I will reward them with a long life
>   and give them my salvation."

This is the covenant of the Lord. The Lord responds to those who respond to Him.

We've been discussing God's answer to those who trust in Him. God always responds to those who stand in faith. The Lord says, *I will rescue you, I will protect you, I will be with you, I will restore you, and I will reward you.* Talk about the "I will's" of God! They are incredible! He rescues those He loves; He will protect those who trust in Him; He will be with those who are trouble; He will answer those who call upon Him; and He rewards them with long life and gives them salvation. What an incredible promise from God! Christ paid for our stress, and He paid for our mental torment so we could live free from mental agitation and worry. We don't have to freak out about the stock market, and we don't have to be freaked out about everybody around us getting laid off. We can have peace in our hearts and our minds, because Christ paid the price. He took your grief; He carried your pain upon the cross.

When Jesus was in the Garden of Gethsemane the Bible says, "He prayed more fervently, and he was in such agony of spirit that his sweat fell to the ground like great drops of blood" (Luke 22:44). Dr. Pierre Barbay of France put together a medical report of the sufferings of Christ. He said, "Though very rare, this phenomenon of *hemotodrosis*, or bloody sweat, is well-documented under great emotional stress like our Lord suffered. Tiny capillaries in the sweat glands can break thus mixing blood and sweat. This process might have well produced marked weakness and possible shock in the body of Jesus." We understand that in Jesus' darkest hour, when He prayed in Gethsemane, He was faced with tremendous pressure—the weight of the world, the sin of the world looming over Him. Jesus asked the Father, "Father, if you are willing, please take this cup of suffering away from me. Yet I want your will to be done, not mine" (Luke 22:42). Even as He agonized, He prayed for the will of the Father, as His blood mingled with His sweat.

Many people have experienced severe medical crisis during this economy. Medical problems are up significantly—specifically stress-induced problems like cardiovascular disease. It's as if people are literally sick of the economy. But Jesus bore in His body our suffering to the highest degree. He took the greatest stress and strain you can imagine on His body. He bore this suffering so we don't have to.

Many of you have been agonizing in prayer, asking God for something, and seeking God's will for some significant breakthrough in your life. Many times you felt like you were alone, and God had gone on vacation! However, it is in those times that we must remember the substitutionary death of our Lord Jesus Christ. He took our place in the area of stress, in the arena where you think your life is out of control, where you feel as though you are not going to be able to put your life back on track and ever recover financially. Jesus went the distance and bore the stress and the strain of it for you. What does that mean? As 1 Peter 5:7 says, "Give all your worries and cares to God, for he cares about you." The literal rendering of that is to throw your care upon the Lord, for the Lord cares for you.

I recently heard about someone who decided he would write everything down that was bothering him, every problem that was a stress in his life. He wrote down twenty-five things. Then he rolled the paper up in a ball, and threw it in the trash. He decided his problems didn't control him any longer. He refused to let those things to be a source of worry and anxiety in his life. Perhaps this is great advice for you. You should do the same—throw your cares, your worries, and your concerns over on the Lord, for He cares for you. He has already borne your stress; He has already borne your anxiety, so why do you continue to bear it? Why do you continue to hold it? God has already given you freedom from things that create pressure in your life. God wants to take you out of that pressure cooker and bring you a season of peace and rest.

Hebrews 4:11 NKJV presents a beautiful picture, saying: "Let us therefore be diligent to enter that rest, lest anyone fall according to the same example of disobedience." The Word speaks of faith *laboring*, standing in faith, using one's faith to trust God and believe in Him. Your faith will bring you into a season of rest. Jesus said, "Let not your heart be troubled: ye believe in God, believe also in me"(John 14:1 KJV). Realign your focus today, and don't allow your life to be tormented one moment longer.

Because we have a covenant with God, there is no room for fear in our lives. The covenant keeps us. The covenant defends us. The covenant speaks on our behalf 24/7, when we are awake, and when we are asleep. We must rest in the strength of the covenant. God cannot fail; He cannot lie. He is almighty God, and He will stand true to His Word.

3
HERE'S A STIMULUS PACKAGE

"The Lord is with me; I will not be afraid.
What can man do to me?"

Psalm 118:6 NIV

What would Jesus say if the Dow Jones dropped 700 points? What would be the response of Scripture? If you have ever played sports before, particularly football, you know what it is like to get the wind knocked out of you. It takes a little while to get your bearings again. With the barrage of negative attacks from the media and other places, it feels like people have gotten the wind knocked out of them. You have to refocus, get your bearings, and say what Jesus would say. Does this affect Jesus? I don't believe that the kingdom of God is moved or affected by the negative financial economy that is going on in our world. Let's focus on the economy of God and not the economy of man.

This is what the Scripture records about God's opinion toward fear. Philippians 1:27-28 NIV says, "stand firm in one spirit, contending as one man for the faith of the gospel without being frightened in any way by those who oppose you." God's instruction to us is to stand firm in one sprit. In other words, you can't be thinking that you are going under one minute and thinking God is going to save you the next minute. You can't be thinking "economic collapse" and that you might have to file bankruptcy one minute and the next minute thinking that God is good and He is going to rescue you from all your problems. Stand firm in one spirit—that is, united with God, being of one mind. We can be double-minded and think a little bit of doubt and little bit of faith, or we can be single-minded and know that God's Word is sure. In this verse it says "with one mind striving together for the faith of the gospel" (KJV)—holding on to what the Word says.

It's difficult to remember the Word of God when your enemies are screaming so loudly at you. But the Bible says to stand in the faith of the gospel, without being frightened in any way by those who oppose you. God cautions us not to be afraid because He is with us, and His Word is working for us.

Another thing you might hear Jesus say is in Romans 8:15: "So you have not received a spirit that makes you fearful slaves. Instead, you received God's Spirit when he adopted you as his own children. Now we call him, 'Abba, Father.'" When we think about what it means to be a son, it opens up a whole new world to us. Anne and I were blessed with three awesome sons. If they need to make a request of me, they know they can always come straight to me and ask. They have the revelation—the spirit of sonship—that we should have so that fear doesn't enslave us. We are not slaves to fear. We understand that Dad will take care of it; it's on Daddy's tab. Dad is going to pick up the check—just as my sons know that if they go out to eat with me, Dad is going to take care of the bill. They can be assured of that. This is not to say that you shouldn't pay your bills, only that God will provide for you.

You might hear Christ say, as Hebrews 13:6 says, "The LORD is my helper, so I will have no fear. What can mere people do to me?" Or as Psalm 118:6 says, "The LORD is for me, so I will have no fear. What can mere people do to me?" What can a negative report do to you? What can increasing layoffs do to you? What can additional foreclosures do to you? The Lord is with you, do not fear. The Creator of the Universe has the remedy and solution. If you will just stay with it and stay focused on God, you are going to win. God is going to bring you through victoriously.

In this chapter I have a stimulus package for you. I want to talk about the power of the kingdom of God. You need to have a revelation of the strength of the kingdom of God before we can proceed in this book. Even though we are in this world, we are not of this world. The people of God are of a different kingdom. Our origin is different, because we have a kingdom that is not shakable. We have received a kingdom that is structured by the hands of God. We need to understand that we operate under a different economic system than the world does. The kingdom of God can break into your world and extend to, through, and above this natural world. Therefore, the kingdom is able to modify our current situations and economic status, because of our trust in the kingdom.

The covenant is exciting for me. It's thrilling, because it's the revelation that we are living in the kingdom of God. The kingdoms of this world have become the kingdoms of His Christ. We live in a superior kingdom. Some of the ways it's described are an *unshakable kingdom* and an *eternal kingdom*, a kingdom of which there is no end. You and I have been born into this incredible entity called the kingdom of God. Let's discuss the power of the kingdom, and how as believers of Christ, we are in this world but not of this world. Even today, before I even began to write, there were more negative news reports. More unemployment benefits are being drawn right now than any time in history. The building of new houses is at an all-time low; it has not been this slow in fifty years. As these negative stats begin to flow, a deep inner faith in every child of God speaks to us and tells us we are not of this world. We are living in the kingdom of God, and although our feet are on this planet, our hearts are connected to God's kingdom, which is over all. The kingdom of God breaks forth into our lives and interrupts the common, natural course of nature.

The laws of God are superior to the laws of men. The laws of the kingdom of God govern the kingdoms of this world. When you activate the laws of the kingdom in your life and you begin to operate in the kingdom, your life takes on a whole different view. You move from despair to victory.

The first thing you have to understand about the kingdom of God is that everything is moved by the King. Everything in the kingdom is moved by the King, our Lord and Savior Jesus Christ by His words. Another thing we understand is that the kingdom of God is neither meat nor drink, but righteousness, peace, and joy in the Holy Spirit (see Romans 14:17). The kingdom of God can affect the natural world, but the essence of the kingdom of God is not natural. The Lord taught us Matthew in 6:33 KJV, "Seek ye first the kingdom of God." He taught us to be kingdom-seekers, to seek the ways and principles of the kingdom.

OPERATING IN KINGDOM PRINCIPLES

We are so familiar with this world and its system that sometimes it's difficult for us to understand how to operate in the kingdom of God. There are so many toxic beliefs in this world that drain us of our spiritual joy and peace. God said the kingdom is not meat nor drink, but righteousness, peace and joy in the Holy Ghost—in that order. When you seek the righteousness of God and His kingdom first, the Bible said that all these things will be added to you. The kingdom of God *can* release things into your life, but the kingdom of God is not based on material things alone.

The kingdom of God is the place where God exercises His might and dominion. It is a realm where the will and the power of the King are expressed. Since we are citizens of the kingdom of God and are submitted to our King, then His will and power is expressed and exercised through us. What comes to mind immediately is that He said, "Beloved, I wish above all things that thou mayest prosper and be in health, even as thy soul prospereth" 3 John 2 (KJV). Our King is a good King. That is one thing we must clearly understand. Our King is a good King, and He loves His people.

In order for there to be a kingdom, there must be a king. The kingdom is based on the rule of the king. His will is sovereign- final. If there were no kingdom, then it would be a republic. A republic is based on the people's choice. But a kingdom is based on the king's will and insight and on His care for the subjects that are in His realm. Thank God we are in the King's "down line!" The full focus of His love and favor is upon you and me, and we are the beneficiaries of our good King's nature.

Our task as citizens of the kingdom is to stay in right standing with the King. Your life must reflect His heart, and you must seek to please the King and get to know His Book. The Word of God contains the laws that govern the kingdom, so we want to live lives that coincide with His laws. This allows us to live in complement to His will. As we do, every decree, favor, and blessing of the King can flow freely to His citizens. Glory be to God!

A powerful passage of Scripture in Matthew 21:21-22 MSG says:

> But Jesus was matter-of-fact: "Yes—and if you embrace this kingdom life and don't doubt God, you'll not only do minor feats like I did to the fig tree, but also triumph over huge obstacles. This mountain, for instance, you'll tell, 'Go jump in the lake,' and it will jump. Absolutely everything, ranging from small to large, as you make it a part of your believing prayer, gets included as you lay hold of God."

Jesus said we have to say yes, we have to embrace the kingdom life. By embracing kingdom life, He said we would overcome our limitations and triumph over huge obstacles. For instance, according to the passage, we would tell the mountain to go jump in the lake! That's why we are not overcome by people who say we are heading for another Great Depression or we are already in a Great Depression. We understand that we are living in the kingdom of God, and we have *chosen* to embrace that. But not everyone will embrace it because not everyone has this insight.

Matthew 13:11 MSG says, "He replied, 'You've been given insight into God's kingdom. You know how it works. Not everybody has this gift, this insight…'" Notice that Jesus says that *insight* is a gift given by God. God gives us the ability to look into His kingdom and understand how it works. When someone has a ready heart, insight and understanding flow freely. That tells us that everyone has access to the gift of insight. We just need our hearts to be ready to hear it.

A ready, willing heart is the key ingredient to having insight and understanding from God flow freely. God first looks at the quality and the character of our hearts. Our hearts have to be in the right place. We are used to dealing with natural things in natural terms. The natural laws that govern this world tell us that 1+1=2; A, B, C, D, E, F, G. We look at things that fit and try to make sense of it all. But to gain insight into the kingdom of God, we have to have hearts ready for change. Our hearts have to readily to accept a different way of living. When Jesus emerged from His forty days of intense trial, tribulation, and temptation from the enemy, He immediately rose up. Matthew 4:17 says, "From then on Jesus began to preach, 'Repent of your sins and turn to God, for the Kingdom of Heaven is near.'" From my studies I have discovered the word "near" is not an appropriate translation from the original Greek. A better translation would be "at hand" or "has arrived." Jesus was saying that from this day forward, the kingdom of God has arrived and that He would proclaim that. The first part is the most vital. The kingdom of God is here; therefore, you are able to access it today. Even in tough economic times, the kingdom of God will cause you to flourish and prosper.

We need to understand how to get this gift of insight. We have already determined from the Scripture that you have to have a ready, expectant heart. Jesus taught that the gateway into kingdom living and kingdom operation is to repent. The word *repent* has been misused in the body of Christ, to the point of almost being misunderstood. The Greek word is the word *metanoia*, and that word carries an incredible weight and strength. *Metanoia* has to do with a mentality change- a mind shift. It means you *change your mind.*

Jesus was saying the kingdom of God has arrived; in other words, it is here today and begins today. All the people at the time were expecting a mighty king to ride in on a white stallion and immediately set up a white throne. They were looking around, wondering where the structure was and where the white horse was. Jesus kept trying to make them understand that this kingdom is spiritual and is made up of spiritual people.

Many people misunderstand the kingdom of God, thinking it is a geographic location. But the kingdom of God is His activity in the lives of His people. In other words, the kingdom of God is not a place; the kingdom of God is an action. It is the will of God being carried out in the lives of His people. This is "Thy will be done on earth, as it is in heaven" every day. One of the benefits of operating in the kingdom is that God will give us insight into business ideas and concepts that can turn our finances completely around.

God provided fresh manna for the children of Israel in the book of Exodus. This is a foreshadowing of Jesus' statement in Matthew 4:4 that man would not live by bread alone but by every word that proceeds from the mouth of God. Insight into the kingdom, the gift of insight, should be something we seek daily. It is something we need daily, just like daily manna for the children of Israel—daily insight, daily Word, daily instruction. Instruction, understanding, and insight are the keys that unlock the power, wealth, and resources of the kingdom of God. According to Deuteronomy 8:18 NIV, this kingdom insight gives us "…the ability to produce wealth, and so confirms his covenant."

The Scripture teaches us so strongly, as Solomon taught in Proverbs 19:8, to love wisdom and cherish understanding. He encourages us to be a lover of Truth, a lover of the Word of God.

Jesus said to get your heart ready, change your mind, and turn to God, for the kingdom of God is at hand right now. Jesus said the kingdom of God has arrived, and masterfully and skillfully taught almost every aspect of life as it relates to the kingdom. Since He was so clear, we have no natural excuse to fall short. We can receive and believe and come into faith concerning the kingdom of God.

Matthew 12:45 MSG says, "You may think you have cleaned out the junk from your lives." I like what one minister says: "You have to get the junk out of your trunk." With a lot of us, this junk is our past issues. Jesus taught that we have to get the junk out of our trunk. We have to get ready for God. There is that word again—get ready for God. He said that people rejected the message of the kingdom, but today the kingdom had arrived. They rejected it because they refused to change their minds and develop a new thought process to operate in God's living kingdom. Jesus said that because they were not hospitable to His kingdom message, all the devils were moving back into their lives.

It is time to get a grip on the kingdom message! Christ said that if you don't embrace the kingdom message, you are on a long bumpy limo ride to nowhere. You think you are going through tough times now. It can get worse for people who reject the good news message that the kingdom of God has come. Our God is alive and well.

Look with me at Ephesians 1:22-23: "God has put all things under the authority of Christ and has made him head over all things for the benefit of the church. And the church is his body; it is made full and complete by Christ, who fills all things everywhere with himself." This Scripture teaches us that the rule of God extends to all, but He has special focus on His own. Our King is a good and gracious King. Let the people rejoice because we have a good King.

Several years ago a friend of mine, Reverend Danny Chambers, had invited me to go on a missionary journey with him to the Cayman Islands. That is such an incredibly beautiful place. One thing that impressed me during the youth conference that he led was how the government had freely given money to churches and youth ministries to reach the young people of the islands. They understood the need was great; they understood that drugs, violence, and teenage suicides were affecting the young people and that the government must step up and do something about it.

That automatically speaks to the kingdom mentality. If you don't live in a kingdom but live in a republic like the United States, it is difficult to understand kingdom mentality. That is why Jesus said you have to change your mind. Even though you might understand natural kingdom mentality, Jesus said My kingdom is going to blow your mind. His kingdom is on a whole new level. Allow this to incubate inside of you. According to Colossians 1:13, "For he has rescued us from the kingdom of darkness and transferred us into the Kingdom of his dear Son." Jesus is the object of the Father's love, and you have been brought into that kingdom. He has included you in the circle of love, and He is treating you like sons and daughters in Christ. He is not treating you according to your sins; He is not treating you according to your actions. He is loving you according to your inheritance; He is loving you according to the love that He has for His dear Son. And thank God, because His dear Son died on the cross for us as the substitutionary Lamb of God who died for our sins. You and I benefit as God's sons and daughters, because Jesus is the object of the Father's love. Jesus died in our stead and brought us in so we can become, and we have become, the object of the Father's love.

Understand you are in the kingdom, and you have been rescued from the domination of darkness, the things that govern this world. Think of what governs this world: greed, the "get all I can get" mentality. Many of the people who were very greedy and materialistic have been greatly humbled. They have lost the majority of their assets because they invested in toxic assets, and have seen their fortunes dwindle before their eyes. Many have come to a deeper understanding that their trust cannot be in material things.

You have to make this mind shift. God's kingdom is not based on greed or selfishness. It is based on *selflessness*. The kingdom of God is not an economy based on fear or hoarding up because of fear. The kingdom of God is a structure based on giving. As we give, we advance; as we release, we move ahead. The world says to hold on to move ahead. God teaches us to release in order to advance. You can see the contrast immediately. That is just a little, tiny slice, a micro-piece of the entire vision of the kingdom of God.

During that incredible crusade in the Cayman Islands, governmental officials were on the platform with us during a full-on, very spiritual meeting and preaching of the gospel. Their presence there confirmed that they supported it. It is just a common understanding in kingdom structure: we take care of our own. It is a negative reflection on the king, if someone is bound or addicted to drugs in the kingdom, if someone is impoverished and is living in poor conditions, and if their clothes are torn or tattered. If they are improperly clothed, fed, or cared for, that is a negative reflection on the king. You have the right and the responsibility to prosper!

One thing we can immediately understand about kingdom structure is that our King loves us, and He has sworn to take care of us. Praise God! I will not fear, because I am living in the kingdom of God, and I have assurance that my King reigns. The King is on the throne, and He reigns. Because of our allegiance to the King and living in submission to the King, the kingdom of God breaks into our natural world. It circumvents and supersedes natural laws to get involved in His people's lives.

People who come into our church start understanding kingdom principles and make statements like the following. To them, the principles about giving and stewardship do not make natural sense. "I am giving away more than I have ever given away, yet I have more at the end of the month than ever before. It does not make mathematical sense," they will say. That is because God's economy is not a mathematical equation; it's *supernatural*. God is able to bring resources down from the heavens. He is able to bring it from the ground up. He is able to materialize it. He is the Creator. God is an innovator. God is not in a rut; He loves to bless and surprise His people. God is unchanging – His desire to give us the best is a permanent trait. He loves to bless us and surprise us. He loves to come out of left field with something we were not even expecting or looking for. He loves to see the delight of a child in us, to see our eyes sparkle and our hearts beat with joy. God loves to see that glow on His children's faces, because He is so incredibly in love with us.

Some people struggle with this because when they look around them, they see so much negativity in our world; they see suffering and tragedy. We want to ask why. Yet we must remember that God has granted access to insight to every individual who will ready his or her heart. But not every heart is ready for that, and that's not God's fault. His will is for all to have this incredible life experience, but we live in a very hostile world. There are opposing forces to your prosperity and advancement. That is why we emphasize that God has rescued us (Colossians 1:13) from the dominion of darkness.

Darkness does not dominate our lives any longer. He brought us into this new kingdom. We see the contrasting forces: the warring factions of this greedy world compared to the kingdom of God, dominated and driven by benevolence, and by a ready heart. Get your mind right. Your thoughts concerning the kingdom of God will definitely determine the measure of blessing you receive.

We had a work day the other day at our church. The associate pastor, Carl Flowers, and I had gone out to take some items to the landfill. While we were unloading the trailer we noticed a gentleman who looked as if he was tugging on stumps from a pile of useless wood. We sat there, and I began to laugh, and then I laughed harder, and I began to make fun of what the man was doing. Pastor Carl began to chime in with me. We could not figure out what was going on—one stump, two stumps. Then all of a sudden we realized that while we were unloading one branch at a time from our trailer, this man was looking for an anchor that he could use to pull his whole load off at one time. Soon enough, he found a long stump that would not move, and when he took off in his truck the whole pile came off at one time. Many times while we are judging others for their activities, we are the ones who come up short. There is always another level of thought; another level to operate in that you are not currently aware of. God rewards a reacher. He wants us to lift our vision higher to see His way of operation.

WHAT IS THE KINGDOM OF GOD?

A Place of Gathering

In the book of Matthew alone, Jesus goes through series of descriptions of the kingdom of God. Over and over, He uses the term "the kingdom of God is like..." Jesus was offering some incredible metaphors. There is no way that the kingdom of God can be summed up in one statement. The kingdom of God is so vast and so incredibly eternal that Christ spent His entire ministry giving us windows of insight into the kingdom and into its operation upon the earth. Jesus would say things like this: the kingdom of God is like a wedding where no guests came (Matthew 22:1-14), but the lord of the feast sent out the servants to go and gather the people from the highways and the side streets and get them to come in. So we understand immediately that the kingdom of God is all-inclusive. It's about gathering, and putting others first. The kingdom of God is a feast, a celebration, a place of joy and merriment, but it is also a place of inclusion.

A Place of Preparedness

Christ, continuing this picture in Matthew 25:1-4 NIV, says, "At that time the kingdom of heaven will be like ten virgins who took their lamps and went out to meet the bridegroom. Five of them were foolish and five were wise. The foolish ones took their lamps but did not take any oil with them. The wise ones, however, took oil in jars along with their lamps." Jesus said that is what the kingdom of God is like. Immediately we can see that Jesus says the kingdom of God is a place of *preparedness*. The oil in the kingdom of God alludes to the anointing of the Holy Spirit. The kingdom of God is where we receive our oil, the strength to live our daily lives that lights our candle for the world. When we are living in the kingdom of God and are under the King's protection, living lives that are pleasing to Him, our hearts are prepared and run over with fresh oil, and we light the way. Kingdom people are innovators and creators. There are people reading this book who will start new businesses in the midst of a slumping economy, because the kingdom of God is a place of innovation. The kingdom is a place where innovators are born. It is where creativity flows; it is where witty inventions and ideas flow.

A Place of Sowing and Reaping

Matthew 13:24 continues the illustration and says the kingdom of God is like a farmer. A farmer sows seed and the field reproduces what is sown in it. Jesus said the kingdom of God is like a farmer- it will reproduce what is sown in it. The kingdom of God will incubate your seed, and release it back into your life in a form that is adequate to meet your need. God will take the material things that we do in His name, and will bring back spiritual answers as a result of the material seeds that we sow. The kingdom of God will produce what you sow into it.

Then He said in Matthew 13:31, "The Kingdom of Heaven is like a mustard seed." Seed goes into the ground and takes on a different form, and the seed has the power to reproduce in itself. Every seed is programmed to be played back at a later date. Every seed has a unique assignment according to the nature of the seed. The kingdom of God is where you discover the power of sowing and reaping. You sow your life and you reap God's strength. You sow your time and you reap God's season. You sow your resources and reap God's supply. God causes the seed that we sow to reproduce. It becomes what we need it to be and takes on the form that we need it to take on.

A Place of Commitment

Jesus said in Matthew 13:44 that "The Kingdom of Heaven is like a treasure that a man discovered hidden in a field." The kingdom of God has great wealth. We find this incredible treasure and when we buy the field (the kingdom), we inherit the treasure. Jesus taught us that we have to be committed to the kingdom, and the kingdom lifestyle. You can't just try it on for a season. You give your life to Jesus when you are born again. To be born again means to be born from above. You are born into the kingdom of God, and in this kingdom you have certain rights and privileges to operate and exercise the will of the King. You have to buy the field, commit to the field, and commit to the treasure. Make a "down payment." The measure of trust and commitment that you invest, will be the measure of reward that you will get back.

There is great reward for those who will buy the field and buy into the things that Jesus asks us to do. He said in the Word to take up our cross and follow Him daily. We can put the negatives of the past behind us, and take up the cross and be totally focused and committed. The cross is a symbol of commitment and responsibility and when we take up the cross, we are walking in His steps and are walking in the realm of blessing. It is a realm of increase and multiplication.

A Place of Discernment

Jesus went on to say in Matthew 13:47 that "Again, the Kingdom of Heaven is like a fishing net that was thrown into the water and caught fish of every kind." When fishermen pull in the net, they find that some fish are desirable and other fish are undesirable. Those undesirable fish are to be culled out, and the edible fish are to be kept and harvested. So we understand that the kingdom of God is a place of *discernment*. It is a place of distinction. When you are walking in the kingdom, God will give you spiritual discernment to know what to separate out, what not to include, what not to be joined to, what relationships to be involved in, and what relationships not to be involved in. God will give you supernatural wisdom in knowing what *to* do, and what *not* to do.

A Place of Equal Opportunity

In Matthew 20:1-16, Jesus said the kingdom of God is like an estate manager who hired some workers. They were all hired at different hours of the day, but they all received equal pay. Here we can see that the kingdom of God is without discrimination. The Scripture teaches that the kingdom of God is a place for everyone, and there is something in the kingdom for everyone. The King loves all the citizens of the kingdom equally, and He wants all of them to receive and be blessed. We all work at different talent and ability levels, yet the kingdom of God is a place where everyone can prosper. Everyone can be blessed in the kingdom of God. You can't say that this one is more qualified or that one has a degree or this individual is more skilled. Praise God, if you are operating in the kingdom, the blessings flow equally in the commonwealth of the kingdom of God. You and I have access to the kingdom of God, and we ought to claim our commonwealth every day. We need to remember that everything in the kingdom realm is moved by words. That is why Jesus said that you can say to the mountain, jump in the lake, and it will, when you operate in the power and the strength of the kingdom of God. The spoken word is the seed at work.

In 2009, President Obama declared that the economy was going to make a turnaround, but it hadn't yet. Just the hint of good news caused the stock market to rise more than two hundred points in one day. That is the power of one positive word. How much more powerful is a word spoken in faith from the Word of God!

In Matthew 18, the disciples were arguing about greatness and rank in the kingdom of God, and Jesus shifted their mindset in a hurry. He began to talk about becoming like a child. In Matthew 18:4 MSG, He says, "Whoever becomes simple and elemental again, like this child, will rank high in God's kingdom." Jesus taught us to

71

go back to the basics. He told us to think with an open mind and trusting heart as a child does. We need to trust our Father to provide everything we need through His incredible kingdom. Jesus declared in Matthew 4:17 that the kingdom had arrived. This was directly after His encounter with the prince of darkness in His forty-day period of being tested and tempted by the enemy. This marked the beginning of a kingdom, a new way of operation. A new way of conducting our lives had begun.

CONQUERING THE PRINCE OF GREED

Think of Jesus' forty-day tempting period in a different light. Before He could declare the kingdom of God, He had to conquer the prince of greed first. In our lives, before we can become child-like and have kingdom blessings prevail in our lives, we have to first encounter the prince of greed, materialism, and lust in our own lives. Then we can truly declare that money does not have a stronghold over us, but that our lives are governed by the kingdom of God. This is a battle we must fight and win before the kingdom can really take control of our lives.

Luke 4:5-8 says,

> Then the devil took him up and revealed to him all the kingdoms of the world in a moment of time. "I will give you the glory of these kingdoms and authority over them," the devil said, "because they are mine to give to anyone I please. I will give it all to you if you will worship me."
>
> Jesus replied, "The Scriptures say, 'You must worship the LORD your God and serve only him.'"

From the beginning, Satan has been competing with God for our devotion. He competes in the arena of our worship and tries to be God's rival. He tries to steal our worship by taking our words of praise, trying to take the place of God in our devotion. Satan would like to steal our devotion to God and replace it with self-worship, the worship of materialism, and the worship of this world. Satan promises authority. The Greek word for authority is *exuosia*. Here, the enemy promises the authority of the kingdoms of the world if Jesus would worship Him. Today, the enemy still promises authority, *exuosia*, to those who would sell their souls and work their fingers to the bone, doing whatever they have to do to get ahead in life. Most scholars agree that in Matthew 4:8-10, Satan manifests himself in yet another way. Here the promise is an emphasis on things, not on the authority of kingdoms, but the things that kingdoms have to offer—materialism. It is a different temptation. In Luke, the temptation is authority and influence. In Matthew, the temptation is things—more toys, more gadgets to fill our lives to distract us from God's purpose. Again, God wants us to have things, but God does not want things to *have us*.

In Jesus' temptation we see an incredible intense attack on His soul and character. Jesus uses different words in Matthew's account than He used in Luke 4, when He says, "Get behind Me, Satan." He was able to put the temptation of influence and the false promise of authority behind Him. But in Matthew 4, when Satan comes and promises materialism and all the things that this world can offer, Jesus changes His response and uses the Greek word *hupage*, which means "go, go from me, get out of my presence," signaling that the test is over. At some point, every believer has to take a stand and refuse to sell out to the spirit of materialism, greed, and false authority, and say, *Hupage!*, "go" to these things—*Get out of my presence! You have no right to govern my life! You have no place in my life at all!*

The day that we decide to build our lives God's way becomes the greatest day of freedom for us. Remember that the kingdom of God does not indicate a place but rather the activity of God in us. He is building something in us that is greater than material wealth, greater than influence, greater than authority. He is building His life in us, and we have to choose to allow that life to be built so that our lives will be on the right foundation.

Jesus teaches in Matthew 4, that building your life on the kingdom of God is building on the right foundation. One man chose to build his life on sand, not taking the time to dig deep and find the bedrock and build his life on the right foundation. He went the route of convenience, picking the quick and easy route, and when the winds and the storms came, the house fell. But there was another man who built his house on bedrock. He dug down and took the extra time and expense to build his house on rock. When the storms of life descended upon it, they were not able to move the house from its foundation. That is the way our lives should be. We must take the extra time to build our lives around God and the things that please Him, and realize that what He is building in us is more significant than what we are trying to build by ourselves. When we let Him build in us, the things that He builds will withstand the storms that this life brings against us.

Jesus' announcement of the new kingdom was an announcement of change—a time to change our minds, a time to go a new direction with our lives. In the old story of the mouse and the maze, a scientist ran an experiment on a mouse, placing him in a maze with some cheese at the end. Every day the mouse would speedily work through the maze to get the cheese at the end. The mouse would do this over and over and over again. After a while, the scientist removed the cheese, and for a day or two the mouse still scurried quickly to the end of the maze. As soon as the mouse realized that there was no cheese at the end, it would just sit there and not move. The mouse had enough sense to know that the cheese had been removed. Perhaps the mouse had more sense than most humans do! The mouse knew that when the cheese had been moved, it was time for change.

All our lives we have depended on certain things, and we have lived our lives by certain values. But what Christ came to declare in His new kingdom was basically that the cheese had been moved, and if we keep looking for satisfaction in the same places we looked for satisfaction before, we are going to come up empty and disappointed. Our old world tactics are no longer working, so it's time to change direction and try His tactics.

QUALITIES THAT BRING BLESSINGS

In Matthew 5, Jesus taught the qualities that bring blessings for those who live in the kingdom of God. The Greek word *markarios* means happy and blessed: Christ said that the person who has these attributes and walks in these qualities is *markarios*. So let's look at these different attitudes.

Jesus taught that those who are blessed in the kingdom of God are going to have the attribute of being "poor in spirit." A person who is *poor in spirit* contrasts with those who walk outside the kingdom of God in their own self-confidence or self-reliance. Jesus taught that *those who mourn* are blessed versus the pleasure-seeking, "beautiful people" of this world. Jesus taught that the *meek* are blessed versus the proud and arrogant, the self-confident of this world. Jesus taught that those who *hunger for righteousness* are blessed versus those who are satisfied within themselves—the non-seeker. Jesus taught that the *merciful* are blessed versus the self-righteous of this world. Jesus taught that the *pure in heart* are blessed versus the secular and the worldly. Jesus taught that the *peacemakers* are blessed versus the aggressive. Jesus taught *those who are persecuted* are blessed versus the popular.

These are the attitudes that bring blessing. Jesus taught that a child of the kingdom should robe himself in these attitudes. To have meekness of heart means we have yielded the authority of our life to God. We are not to be proud and arrogant and self-assured. Every trait Jesus taught—mercy, pureness of heart, peacemaker, and those who are poor in spirit yet are enriched by God's presence within them—is exactly the opposite of what the world tells us to be. But to operate in the kingdom of God and access the great wealth that the kingdom affords to every yielded child of God, we have to robe ourselves in these attitudes. These are the qualities that will bring blessings in our lives.

TOXIC ASSETS

I've mentioned a term before: *toxic assets*. Greg Larson, editor of preachingtoday.com, wrote that the 2009 economic crisis brought this interesting phrase into the headlines.

Toxic assets contribute to the recent mess that the banks are in. The assets are loans that people owe to the banks. Normally banks *want* people to owe them money and pay them interest on the principal. But as the economy now stands, especially with the mortgage foreclosure crisis, many of the loans have become liabilities, because the houses that secured the loans have decreased in value below the amount of the loan. When assets become harmful to your bottom line, they are no longer assets. They are liabilities; they are toxic.

Toxic assets are not just a banking phenomenon. A toxic asset can also be spiritual. This could be anything we think of as an asset but is actually hurting us spiritually. Sins of the flesh, such as viewing pornography or taking illegal drugs, are toxic assets. We engage in these pleasures because we think they will benefit us, but the opposite is true. A house or a car can be a toxic asset when it takes over your life and pushes God to the periphery. A job can be a toxic asset; so can money, education, family and friends, physical beauty or handsomeness. These things can be great assets to you until you allow them to overtake God's place in your life, and you begin to live for them or trust in them. When that happens, they have become toxic assets.

That powerful article teaches us that we need to close the door to the toxic assets in our lives. Jesus taught us how to form the behavior of the kingdom of God by telling us not to allow our hearts to be corrupted by greed or to center on the things that we possess. Jesus was very clear that a man's life does not consist of the things he has. Our hearts should find value in our relationship with God. This is the number one key for the true kingdom-seeker: don't let your heart to get bogged down with insignificant things, instead focus on your relationship with God.

In Matthew 6:19-21, Jesus said, "Don't store up treasures here on earth, where moths eat them and rust destroys them, and where thieves break in and steal. Store your treasures in heaven, where moths and rust cannot destroy, and thieves do not break in and steal. Wherever your treasure is, there the desires of your heart will also be." We are really talking about priorities. What do you treasure? What do you value? God teaches us not to place our value in material things. Don't overrate your stuff, but trust in the kingdom of God. When we are good stewards over the resources God gives us, we are storing up riches in heaven. Our future is protected. Talk about insurance! Our future assets are protected by heaven, and there will come a day when we need to make a withdrawal. We will not have to worry about being protected by the FDIC. Heaven will open up its treasure to us and yield the blessings and provision we need when a crisis arises. We have something deposited in the heavenly bank. He says that moth and rust cannot destroy and thieves do not break in and steal. Verse 21 says that wherever your treasure is, there the desires of your heart will also be. Keep your heart in the right place, because your heart will always lead you to treasure.

VISION

We have heard it said that "where there is vision, there will be provision." Whatever desire God put in your heart, God will finance. God will provide the treasure to fulfill the desire, which is really Him fulfilling His dream through you. God will use people to establish His will here on earth. He places desires in the hearts of His people for the things that He wants to see happen. These people with desire act upon the Word of God, and God will finance the desire, because it is from Him.

Matthew 6:22,23 says, "Your eye is a lamp that provides light for your body. When your eye is good, your whole body is filled with light. But when your eye is bad, your whole body is filled with darkness. And if the light you think you have is actually darkness, how deep that darkness is!" This is a very interesting, intriguing passage of Scripture. Dr. Roy Blizzard, a past professor at the University of Texas and an expert in Greek studies, says that the actual rendering is something like this, "If a man's eye is filled with lack, then his whole body will act accordingly. All of his life will fall in line with the vision that he sees. If his eye is miserly and always sees just barely getting by or barely enough, then the rest of his life will reflect what he sees." But he said there is a phrase in the Greek that translates "if his eye is abundant" and "abundant eye." If his eye is abundant then his whole life will be filled with abundance. Abundance will come.

It all comes back to vision regulating life. God wants to flood our lives with light. He wants to fill our lives with resources. But we choose our vision. We must not allow our vision to be corrupted by a world that is screaming "Not enough!" and "We can barely make it!" and so on. We can't allow our personal visions to be contaminated by the negative reports of this world.

One rendering says that if we focus on things alone, the light of God's revelation will be blocked out and our whole personality will be darkened. We need to allow our vision to be expanded, because our vision will regulate the rest of our lives. If our vision is abundant, then our lives will be filled with abundance. If our vision is just barely getting by, then our lives will respond accordingly. Praise God! It does not cost us anything at all to change our vision—just our attitudes and what we allow to formulate them. We can work on our vision right now by allowing God's Word to change us. We can change our lives by changing our vision.

Sometimes it is not a matter of just having the facts. Someone always says, "Pastor Moore, the facts are the facts." Well, sometimes there is a higher level of knowledge than what we have. In Dr. Phil Pringle's book, *Keys to Financial Excellence*, he talks about having a God-sized vision. He said that everybody is talking about how we are going to run out of things and the earth does not have enough supply and on and on. He said in the next twenty years, the global population will extract the following from the earth's natural resources: $220 billion worth of copper, $50 trillion worth of gold, $300 billion worth of silver, $360 billion worth of aluminum, $600 billion worth of iron, tin, zinc, and lead; $16 trillion worth of oil; $1.5 trillion worth of barley, $4 trillion worth of corn, $19 trillion worth of meat, $4 trillion worth of rice, $4 trillion worth of pork, and $3.6 trillion worth of wheat.

He goes on to say that among an unbelievable abundance of other things in the earth, there are $80 trillion worth of coal reserves and $600 trillion worth of electrical power reserves. These are just the nature resources of our planet. This doesn't even begin to count the huge wealth in production, machinery, real estate, computers, banking, commerce, and all the other means of wealth generation in the earth. None of these reserves of wealth were meant to be in the hands of the enemy to finance opposition to God's work in the earth. This is God's earth, not the devil's. The wealth of the planet He created belongs in the hands of His children. All the gold, diamonds, and oil have been placed in the earth for the children of God to inherit. His supply is fluid. As it flows through us, it will flow to us.

In Matthew 6:24, Christ goes on to say, "No one can serve two masters. For you will hate one and love the other; you will be devoted to one and despise the other. You cannot serve both God and money." It keeps coming back to where we place our devotion. God is without rival in our lives. We cannot serve God and money; we must serve God exclusively. Money is a tool. It has been given to us to help us fulfill our assignment on the earth. We are not to serve it. Each of us has a unique assignment for our lives; each of us has a unique calling. That money is meant to aid and assist us in our callings. That is a brand-new view; it is definitely not a secular view, it is biblical.

Jesus takes us deeper, as we discover in Luke 16:9. He says, "Here's the lesson: Use your worldly resources to benefit others and make friends. Then, when your earthly possessions are gone, they will welcome you to an eternal home." Christ is clear that the resources that we have are to be used to benefit others, to help others, and to bless others. Fearonomics is an economy that is based on fear and self-preservation, but the kingdom of God is a kingdom based on generosity and giving—radical giving and radical living. Luke 16:10 says, "If you are faithful in little things, you will be faithful in large ones. But if you are dishonest in little things, you won't be honest with greater responsibilities." I believe that God uses money as a test to see if we are faithful in small matters. If we are, then God will make us faithful in larger matters. If we can be faithful with a hundred dollars then God will see if we will be faithful with a thousand dollars or more. He knows that if we will be faithful in small things, then He will be able to entrust greater matters and greater responsibilities to us.

Luke 16:11 says, "And if you are untrustworthy about worldly wealth, who will trust you with the true riches of heaven?" I am convinced that when God speaks of true riches, He is literally talking about true riches. There is no doubt He that is talking about spiritual gifts, assignments, ministry responsibility, harvest, breakthrough, influence, and authority in the kingdom of God. I believe those are the true riches or the greater riches. But first you have to be responsible with worldly wealth. Can you handle worldly wealth? I know some of you are saying, "Give me a chance! Try me, and let's see!" But God wants you to be faithful in the very small things, the minute things of life: paying your bills on time, being honest, paying your taxes, and being faithful to your local church with your tithes and offerings. These are things that God is interested in. If you can be faithful in these areas, then the greater riches of the kingdom will be available to you.

Luke 16:12 says, "And if you are not faithful with other people's things, why should you be trusted with things of your own?" Can you be faithful for your employer? Are you a good worker? Do you use the company's time wisely? Do you use the resources and materials your company gives you to build the company or are you using them for your own advantage? God is never able to give you your own until you are able to take care of somebody else's—and to do that with the same love and attention that you would give to your own business. That is a mark of the kingdom of God. God will honor you and bless you when you take care of somebody else's possessions as if they are your own.

Luke 16:13 says, "No one can serve two masters. For you will hate one and love the other; you will be devoted to one and despise the other. You cannot serve both God and money." Again, emphasis is on your devotion. Where is your worship? From the beginning, the prince of greed has been competing for your devotion and worship. Christ must be without rival in our lives. Our love for Him must be exclusive; it cannot compete with money, things, cars, houses, mansions, land. Nothing else comes before Him.

We are seeing the effects of rampant greed like no other time in history. Mark Galli wrote about the scandal of the AIG bonuses in an article on ChristianityToday.com. He put it this way:

On the surface, it sounds like a healthy company was rewarding its best and brightest. Over 400 employees recently received bonuses. Three-fourths of the company received more than $100,000. Fifty-one employees received $1 to $2 million;

fifteen received more that $2 million, and six received $4 million. The highest bonus stood at $6.4 million.

President Obama said it made him "angry." Comedian Stephen Colbert says he wanted to lead a pitchfork-wielding mob after the execs. Senator Chuck Grassley (R-IA) said the executives should fall on their swords. Representative Paul Hodes (D-NH) says the company's initials now stand for "arrogance, incompetence, and greed." Most of us are mad as Hades and aren't going to take it anymore. It's a scandal, a national folly, and we want our money back.

The outrage at the incomprehensible unfairness of it all seems most appropriate as we walk through the most reflective of church seasons.

We are in the middle of Lent, treading water in the muddy pool of self-examination. We see a lot of muck and mud as we look within. The harder we look, the darker things are. At the bottom of this bottomless pool, toward which we are rapidly sinking, lurks death. And dragging us down is nothing but our own arrogance, incompetence, and greed.

When it comes to self-reflection, the Bible writers seem to live in a perpetual Lent. Paul said that humans are "filled with all unrighteousness, wickedness, greed, evil; full of envy, murder, strife, deceit, malice; they are gossips, slanderers, haters of God, insolent, arrogant, boastful, inventors of evil, disobedient to parents, without understanding, untrustworthy, unloving, unmerciful" (Romans 1:29-31 NASB). The prophet Jeremiah said, "The heart is more deceitful than all else and is desperately sick; Who can understand it?" (Jeremiah 17:9 NASB). This sort of behavior makes you angry if you spot it in others. What makes some even more angry is when that behavior seems to get rewarded. Paul, however, speaks of God's reward. Romans 5:15-16 NASB says:

> But the free gift is not like the transgressor. For if by the transgression of the one the many died, much more did the grace of God and the gift by the grace of the one Man, Jesus Christ, abound to the many. The gift is not like that which came through the one who sinned; for on the one hand the judgment arose from one transfression resulting in condemnation, but on the other hand the free gift arose from many transgressions resulting in justification.

More to the point, "…God demonstrates His own love toward us, in that while we were yet sinners, Christ died for us." (Romans 5:8 NASB).

The Bible does not tell us how to handle the AIG bonus crisis, but it does tell us about the nature of the gospel. The people who have brought a busload of problems on themselves and the planet are the very people who are offered the bonus of redemptive grace. It's a mercy for the likes of us foolish, faithless, heartless, ruthless people who receive the salary of common grace, but now a bonus of saving grace is offered to those on a scale few could image possible. Who can understand it?

Human greed gets us into a lot of trouble, but God's grace frees us from ourselves and gives us heaven's perspective as to how we ought to live. Jesus alluded to this in Matthew 13:41 when He said that we should remove everything that is offensive from His kingdom. We are responsible for removing the offensive stuff from within us, the things that oppose the kingdom's ability to work through us. In the areas where we trusted ourselves, we need to trust God and His plans for our lives.

This teaching on the kingdom of God is best summed up in Hebrews 12:26-29:

> When God spoke from Mount Sinai his voice shook the earth, but now he makes another promise: "Once again I will shake not only the earth but the heavens also." This means that all of creation will be shaken and removed, so that only unshakable things will remain.
>
> Since we are receiving a Kingdom that is unshakable, let us be thankful and please God by worshiping him with holy fear and awe. For our God is a devouring fire.

There are a couple of points to notice. First of all, God promises that everything that can be shaken will be shaken, and only unshakable things will remain. We must examine our lives and our hearts. How are we geared? How are we wired? Are we established on unshakable things? These are the things that are based on the kingdom of God, based on the behavior patterns that Christ set forth for you and me: humility, meekness, pleasing God, and using the wealth and resources He gave us to serve others. This is the true and right kingdom mindset, the mindset that will never be shaken. As He said, since we have received a kingdom that is unshakable, those who operate within it are unshakable individuals.

We are living in very unstable times, but we should be encouraged that we are anchored in the Rock, Jehovah, and that our lives are established in God. The emphasis, as the writer of Hebrews concludes, is to be thankful and to worship God and God alone with holy awe. Let your passion burn strong for God, that your life would always be in line with His standards.

An old naval vessel was turning in the waters and saw a bleep on the radar screen. Immediately they sent out a message that they were a U.S. Naval vessel, and the other vessel had to turn its course from the current heading. There was silence on the other end of the radio transmission, and the commander said again, more forcefully this time, "This is a U.S. Naval vessel, and we command you to change your heading, or you will be struck." Again, the radio was silent. He said, "For the last time, change your course at once. This is a U.S. Naval vessel, and I am commanding you to change your course." Finally a voice came over the radio: "This is a lighthouse, and we would urge you to change your course at once."

So many times we buck God's standards, trying to get Him to change course, when we are the ones who need to change course. When we put our lives on course with the kingdom and the teachings that Christ gave us, then our lives will be brighter than before. Our futures will be brighter than ever, because we are in the kingdom which cannot be shaken no matter how troubled the times become. God's kingdom will not be shaken.

4

A BAILOUT FOR ALL
GENERATIONS

———————◆———————

[The Lord instructed the children of Israel,] "You must not worship any of the gods of the neighboring nations."

Deuteronomy 6:14

In a recent article in *Men's Health* magazine titled "The Wealth-Building Kit," writer Richard Sign asked:

> What do you do when your stock portfolio evaporates, your job disappears, and the debt collectors start pounding at your door? Maybe you apply sheer determination and work as many hours at as many jobs as you can. Your buddy, by contrast, may shut himself in his apartment and ponder jumping out the window. Your brother may sell all his worldly possessions and trek through India in search of his true calling. And Donald Trump? He will just double down again and again until he hits another lucky streak. Your reaction to financial stress depends on the way you view the world, and experts in the science of personality say that these reactions are predictable.

It really does come down to how we view the world. Or perhaps our reactions are not so much dependent on how we view the world but on how we view our God. So many times we make God so small, and we make our problems so large, when we should microsize our problems and supersize our view of God. A great way to do this is to speak the Word over our lives.

The faithfulness of God is something every believer should use as an anchor for their lives. Our God is faithful; He has been faithful to every generation. He will continue to be faithful to those who place their trust and their strength in Him. Starting with Exodus through the book of Deuteronomy, before the Jews entered their Promised Land, the Bible said that God's character and nature would be passed down from one generation to the next. Then the next generation would always know God as their source, their helper, their deliverer, the one who would supply all of their needs.

In *The Message* Bible, Isaiah 38:18-19 says,

> The dead don't thank you,
>   and choirs don't sing praises from the morgue.
> Those buried six feet under
>   don't witness to your faithful ways.
> It's the living—live men, live women—who thank you,
>   just as I'm doing right now.
> Parents give their children
>   full reports on your faithful ways.

We are encouraged about our futures and our destinies, and have an awesome reality of the faithfulness of God. Parents who have a deep relationship with God pass on stories of God's faithful ways to their children and generations to come.

Personally, I thank God for the legacy of faith in my life. My Grandmother Taylor was a very devoted woman of God, a prayer warrior who handed down many testimonies of God's faithfulness. God provided for her and her family through very lean, tough times. My father grew up during the Depression and passed down wonderful testimonies of God's grace and mercy. These are full reports of God's faithfulness. I know today that my life is better because of these stories. I am encouraged to pass that faith down to my children, because God showed faithfulness from generation to generation.

In this time of transition in this country, many families are going through a transition as well. You are going from one season to another, one job to another job, one level of income to another level of income. The way you handle this transition is important. Keep your God vision in the right place as your circumstances change.

Let's look closely at the children of Israel as they were preparing to enter the Promised Land. They were getting ready to enter a new season. The way this transition would occur, and the way it was to be explained to the people through Moses was critical in the heart and mind of God. There would be some key elements given to the next generation so they could preserve an understanding of God's faithfulness and continue to see God as supplier and God of increase.

GOD IS YOUR FIRST PRIORITY

God passed down some critical steps through Moses to the children of Israel. The first was in Deuteronomy 6:5-7: "And you must love the LORD your God with all your heart, all your soul, and all your strength. And you must commit yourselves wholeheartedly to these commands that I am giving you today. Repeat them again and again to your children. Talk about them when you are at home and when you are on the road, when you are going to bed and when you are getting up." The first step is that we must *give God priority.* We are passing this on to the next generation. The number one step that parents should teach their children is to love God. Love God with all their hearts, with all of their souls, with all of their strength, and with all of their understanding. In order for that to happen, the Israelites were supposed to talk about it: when they sat at home, when they walked along the road, when they lay down at night, and when they got up in the morning. They would constantly rehearse the love of God, the love that they had for God, and the love that God had for them. God was not speaking about memorization alone but about a much deeper truth. The passage calls on us to make God's Word a part of our lives: to let His teachings reshape our values, our attitudes, and our behavior.

I am reminded of the inventors of the game Monopoly, which was created during the Depression. Before the Depression, the creators of the game had wealth, but they had lost it all. However, they began to catch a vision for the future. *What are we going to do to survive the Depression?* they asked. They talked about what they would do if they had the money to do it, and they began to dream. They sat around the kitchen table and dreamed and talked about where they would go and what they would do with the money if they were in better times after the Depression ended. They made a game of it and began to exchange play money. The activity became so popular that friends would come over and play and dream about what they would buy and what they would invest in and what they would do. Out of that simple exchange of ideas, a board game was created. Parker Brothers eventually bought it for a million dollars. They dreamed and discussed their way into a better life.

God wants His people to do the same—to discuss and rehearse what the future will look like when your blessings and finances come in. Don't pout, and don't complain about how bad things are. Begin to rehearse how good things are going to be. God asked His people to pass this love for God on. He was mentally preparing them for a day beyond the manna, beyond the judgments in Egypt, beyond the fiery clouds and the victory at Moab. He said that they would have to be able to communicate the goodness of God to the next generation.

The greatest fear is that God's people would enter a season produced by God but forget that God had done it. They would forget to give glory to God. For the most part, in America we are in this exact position, where we have come through a season of goodness and prosperity and plenty. But instead of passing on the values like hard work and loyalty that contributed to our prosperity, we've passed on things like gadgets, PlayStations, and GameBoys. Don't forget to teach your children to love God and to value God as the priority above all else.

GOD IS WITH YOU

The next thing they were to do was *trust in God's presence.* God's presence is the equalizer in our lives. God causes things to happen. If we live our lives in union with Him and His Word, then His presence will be with us. His presence in us opens doors. It causes favor to go ahead of us. It is what causes your résumé to go to the top of the stack. It is what causes the boss to consider you for a raise over everyone else. The presence of God makes incredible things happen in your life.

In Deuteronomy 6:14-19, the Lord instructed the children of Israel,

"You must not worship any of the gods of neighboring nations, for the LORD your God, who lives among you, is a jealous God. His anger will flare up against you, and he will wipe you from the face of the earth. You must not test the LORD your God as you did when you complained at Massah. You must diligently obey the commands of the LORD your God—all the laws and decrees he has given you. Do what is right and good in the LORD's sight, so all will go well with you. Then you will enter and occupy the good land that the LORD swore to give your ancestors. You will drive out all the enemies living in the land, just as the LORD said you would."

God wanted His people to trust exclusively in His presence. Even though they had seen great signs and wonders, at Massah they had assumed that the Lord was not with them. They had tested the Lord in asking whether the Lord was with them or not. Their instructions were to *assume* that God's presence was with them. They were not to put their faith in the foreign gods of neighboring nations. They were not to trust in their idols or their methods.

Again we can come back to the teaching on the kingdom of God. If we are following God's principles—and refuse to be confused with the greed, hate, indifference, and unethical practices that govern the world's way of doing business—then we are following God's design and trusting in His presence. In Deuteronomy 18:9, God told the Israelites not to imitate the customs of others when He said, "When you enter the land the LORD your God is giving you, be very careful not to imitate the detestable customs of the nations living there." In other words, don't conform to the ways of the world. Don't go back to trusting in your own ability. Don't go back to trusting in your own strength, but trust in the Lord. His presence will be with you, will make the difference in the land. God said He would drive out the enemies before them. When you do what is right and good in the Lord's sight, things will go well for you. Use the instructions that He has given in His Word. These instructions brought the Israelites to the Promised Land, and continued helping them to flourish, prosper, and increase in the new season that God had for them. The presence of God would be with them. Don't bow down to the strange idols, He told them. Their hearts were to be truly devoted to God. Their worship was to be exclusive for Him.

History tells us that many people believed in the false gods named Baal. They would set up altars throughout their land. They believed the Baal gods would bring blessing and increase, and cause their crops to flourish. They believed that certain Baal gods ruled over specific geographic areas and caused the crops to produce a greater yield. One of God's instructions was not to worship the Baal gods. The Lord wanted to be the exclusive source of blessing for His people. He wanted them to know that He was the one who caused the land to be fruitful, and multiply. No one but Him: "Thou shalt have no other gods before me" (Exodus 20:3 KJV). Only He, only El Shaddai, the God of more than enough, would cause the land to produce for them.

God calls for that same trust today. It is our God and His presence that will cause the land to produce a greater yield. It is imperative that we are led by the Holy Spirit and not pressured by others, and that we don't conform just because of what other people are doing. Other people might be pulling out of investments, while God may be telling you to invest in a certain thing. We definitely follow different guidelines than everyone else. We follow the guideline of the Holy Spirit. God will tell you where to invest, how to invest, and which investments will yield the greatest return.

Let's assume the presence of God. Let's rely on the presence of God. Even though times are tough, trust! Do not question whether the Lord is with you or not. Know that He is with you, because He said so. He is the one who causes the land to multiply; He is the one who causes your life to be productive and to grow vigorously. He is the one who causes your business to grow vigorously and the work of your hand to prosper, according to Deuteronomy 28:8 NIV: "The LORD will send a blessing on your barns and on everything you put your hand to. The LORD your God will bless you in the land he is giving you."

RELY ON GOD'S PROVISION

The third thing we must do is rely on God's provision. Look at Deuteronomy 6:20-25:

"In the future your children will ask you, 'What is the meaning of these laws, decrees, and regulations that the LORD our God has commanded us to obey?'

"Then you must tell them, 'We were Pharaoh's slaves in Egypt, but the LORD brought us out of Egypt with his strong hand. The LORD did miraculous signs and wonders before our eyes, dealing terrifying blows against Egypt and Pharaoh and all his people. He brought us out of Egypt so he could give us this land he had sworn to give our ancestors. And the LORD our God commanded us to obey all these decrees and to fear him so he can continue to bless us and preserve our lives, as he has done to this day. For we will be counted as righteous when we obey all the commands the LORD our God has given us.'"

Now look at verse 23: "He brought us out of Egypt so He could give us this land he had sworn to give our ancestors." It is important for you to see what He is saying—He brought us out to bring us in. He brought us out of Egypt. Egypt represents bondage, a slave mentality. You could look at it as being enslaved to debt, being a slave of poverty or lack. He said that He brought us out of that so He could give us the land. Many of us have to be brought out of one mindset before we can be brought into an arena of blessing and promotion and help. God has to bring us out of this Egypt mentality today, and we have to start to believe that God has a better land for us. He wants you to experience a different atmosphere. This is what they are passing on to the children-they must rely on God's provision. He brought them out of one mentality to bring them into a new mentality, a new understanding.

The second part of the verse is: "so He could continue to bless us and to preserve our lives." This part of the promise was not only to illustrate that God had provided for their ancestry but also to remember that God would continue to provide. They were to rely on God's continual provision in the generations to come. That has to settle deep within us, as an anchor to our belief system. We have to understand that God is our continual provision.

Deuteronomy 7:9 says, "Understand, therefore, that the LORD your God is indeed God. He is the faithful God who keeps his covenant for a thousand generations and lavishes his unfailing love on those who love him and obey his commands." If we continue to love God, seek Him and worship Him, then to a thousand generations God will continue to be faithful. Sometimes people want to bring up dispensationalism—that these promises were just for the Israelites and are not for us today. But it is clear that God has included us in His covenant provision, which we covered in chapter one. Malachi 1:5 says, "Truly, the LORD's greatness reaches far beyond Israel's borders!" His faithfulness touches and includes our borders and our lives as well.

Deuteronomy 8:18 NKJV says, "And you shall remember the LORD your God, for *it is* He who gives you power to get wealth, that He may establish His covenant which He swore to your fathers, as *it is* this day." The word *remember* is used fifty-three times before the book of Nehemiah in the Old Testament. God urges the people to tell their children to never forget God's goodness. Remember the Lord your God.

God is never surprised by crisis. He prepared His people for a new day, a new time, a new land. They formed a new and unique ethos—a community based on faith and trust in God. This legacy had been passed down from generation to generation, knowing God would surely deliver. This was the same God who had been faithful to bring them out of slavery and fulfill every prophecy that was given to Abraham.

Over a period of four hundred years, God proved His faithfulness. God's people understood that He would deliver; there was no shadow of doubt. They formed a community of faith and trust. The seasons of their lives would change, but they would constantly be reminded that "I am the Lord that changeth not." God would bring them from one season into a new season, reminding them that it was a new day.

These steps prepare you for receiving the blessings of God in this new season. Essentially God said, "Now you are going to have to sow seed in the land, and learn this dimension of My kingdom, that My kingdom will reproduce what you will sow in it." God's people knew they were covenant children of life, and they knew they were uniquely loved by God. That was an understood fact. The circumstances, adversity, and pain would not change the God who they trusted.

The Lord gives this promise in Zephaniah 3:20 to people who have lost so much during our current crisis: "I will give you a good name, a name of distinction, among all the nations of the earth, as I restore your fortunes before their very eyes." Maybe you have lost a large part of your retirement in the stock market, but I am going to believe God. Stay optimistic and declare His Word, that He will restore your fortunes right before your eyes. God can and will do that for those who trust Him.

One young lady was going through some tough times and a lot of adversity. She knew that her mother was a person of faith who prayed and trusted God. She had seen her mother weather a number of storms. She went to her for advice, and as her mother began to maneuver around the kitchen, she grabbed three different things—an egg, a carrot, and some coffee beans. She turned the stove on, placed three pots on it, and began to boil water in each pot. She then placed the egg in one of the pots.

At this point her daughter was wondering what all this had to do with her problem. She had expected her mother to offer some great word of wisdom from the Bible or something from her past to help her out.

Her mother continued what she was doing. She placed the carrot in another pot and some coffee beans in the third pot. After a while she turned all the burners off.

"Let's examine these three things," she said to her daughter.

She took the egg out of the water, cracked it, and pointed out that the egg had hardened in the boiling water.

Then she took the carrot out of the water. In the boiling water, the carrot had become soft and pliable.

Finally, she pointed to the pot of water containing the coffee beans. The beans had changed the composition of the water. The coffee beans themselves were not changed, but in the intense heat of the boiling water they gave off an aroma that changed the atmosphere.

The daughter asked, "What does that have to do with my problem?"

"Well, you have three options when you go through trials," her mother said. "You can become hard and indifferent, you can become pliable and soft and break under pressure, or you can be like those coffee beans and can change your atmosphere."

When we, as children of God, undergo tough and difficult times, there ought to be an aroma of praise and worship that is released from our spirits that changes our atmosphere. That is why I think the children of Israel sang so often. With a song and a shield, they proceeded forth into every battle.

Let's look deeper at this transition and God's faithfulness. Israel had been promised full possession of the land, but with the promise came a warning. Just as God has granted us full possession of His kingdom, the blessings and the privileges come with a disclaimer. In Deuteronomy 9:4 NASB the Lord instructs, "Do not say in your heart when the LORD your God has driven them out before you, 'Because of my righteousness the LORD has brought me in to possess this land.'" God never wanted life to be about our goodness, or righteousness. It is not about a performance of the flesh or about a performance of our spirituality. When you come into the land—and that land could be *whatever* for you, a new job, a new house, answered prayer for a financial blessing—you have to remember that *God* brought you there. Nothing you have is yours. God gave you your sight. He gave you your strength. He gave you the ability to work. He gave you the provision that you have. It all belongs to Him.

Consider this picture of a victorious team. They've just won a championship, and everybody is high fiving and saying, "Look what we've done!" They're celebrating and breaking out champagne bottles and streamers and championship T-shirts. I can also see God warning the people not to say in their hearts that they are righteous. It is not time for high fives and "look what we've done." God brought them into the land. God says that by these instructions you came into the land, and these same instructions are going to keep you in the land. For many people, troubled times are a wakeup call to re-center their values.

In more than twenty-five years in ministry, I have seen people come into the church with great need and distress. They turn their lives over to God, and they start being faithful. They start worshipping God and bringing their families to church on a regular basis. Then the goodness of God starts to overflow in their lives, and with the goodness of God comes freedom and liberty. But they end up even worse than when they started, because somewhere in the process they forget that it is God who brought them better lives.

Looking deeper, we can see that God is a jealous God. The Hebrew rendering of "do not say in your heart my righteousness brought me into the land" portrays a high level of commitment that demands expression. God wants a response from His children. He looks for them to say, "God, Father, You are my source, and my life is committed to You." There must be a corresponding act of faith from us. God is a jealous God, and He wants to receive all the glory. Exodus 20:5 says, "I, the LORD your God, am a jealous God."

Years ago, a gentleman frequently walked a tightrope over Niagara Falls. When he walked the tightrope, thousands would gather to watch him. One day he asked, "How many of you believe I can push this wheelbarrow and walk across this tightrope at the same time?"

Everybody frantically cheered, "Yes, you can!"

So he walked the tightrope, and when he returned to the crowd, he asked if there were any volunteers who wanted to be pushed across the tightrope in the wheelbarrow. Of course, silence hung over the audience. No one wanted to get in the wheelbarrow and let him push them across the Falls. Finally, his assistant—who was employed by him—was the only one to volunteer. Of course, they made it across and back. That shows commitment. It is easy to stand on the sidelines and cheer someone else while they're walking the tightrope. But when it comes down to getting in the wheelbarrow and taking the ride ourselves—well, now we're talking about commitment.

It's like the joke about breakfast: the chicken made a contribution, but the pig made a sacrifice. Nobody wants to make that sacrifice because it requires a life commitment. The Israelites understood they were loved by God. It's similar to the way children understand the love of their parents. Their parents want the best for them and are looking out for their best interests. Our Father, our Daddy in heaven, is looking out for our best interests as well. We have the same assurance that He is looking out for our good.

Psychologist Abraham Maslow said that each individual has two basic needs. Number one is the need for love, and number two is the need for a sense of belonging. As a pastor, I can see that this is absolutely right. That is what church life ought to be about: the reality of love and a sense of belongingness. Church ought to be about including people. When people understand they are included and even celebrated, they tend to rise to their potential.

This is the same way that the laws of prosperity work. These laws have not been talked about a great deal, but the root of prosperity is love, knowing that you are loved and knowing you belong. Perhaps that is why God was able to give and His people were able to receive such lavish blessings. The Israelites knew that God loved them, and also that He had given them many promises as His people. So knowing that you belong, too, is the key to understanding that you are loved and that God's blessing is on your life.

Sky Jethani, author of *The Divine Commodity* (Zondervan 2009), shares the story of a trip he took to India with his father. While he was walking the streets of New Delhi, a little boy approached him. He was as skinny as a rail and wore only a pair of tattered blue shorts. His legs were stiff and contorted, like a wire hanger twisted upon itself. Because of his condition, the little boy could only waddle along on his calloused knees. He made his way toward Sky and his father and cried out, "One rupee, please, one rupee!"

Sky describes what happened when his father eventually responded to the boy's persistent begging.

"What do you want?" his father asked.

"One rupee, sir," the boy said while motioning his hand to his mouth and bowing his head.

The father laughed and said, "How about I give you five rupees?"

The boy's submissive countenance suddenly became defiant. He retracted his hand and sneered at them. He thought the father was joking and having a laugh at his expense. After all, no one would willingly give up five rupees.

The boy began shuffling away, mumbling curses under his breath.

Sky's father reached into his pocket. Hearing the coins jingle, the boy stopped and looked back over his shoulder. Sky's father was holding out a five rupee coin. He approached the boy and placed the coin in his hand. The boy didn't move. He just stared at the coin in his hand.

Sky and his father passed the boy and proceeded to cross the street.

A moment later the shouting resumed—except this time, the boy was yelling, "Thank you! Thank you, sir! Bless you!" He raced after them again—not for more money but to touch Sky's father's feet.

This is how our God sees us—in desperate need of His help. But rather than asking for what we truly need, rather than desiring what He is able and willing to give, we settle for less.

I thought that article was incredible. As I read it, this came up in my heart: *don't settle for less*. Our desire, passion, and hunger ought to match God's ability. How often do we settle for lesser things? The boy was willing to settle for one rupee and could not even imagine that the man was willing to give him five. Sometimes we settle for less when God wants to give us so much more. It all comes back to how much He loves us.

God's amazing provision is evident in 2 Kings 4:1-7 (NIV):

> The wife of a man from the company of the prophets cried out to Elisha, "Your servant my husband is dead, and you know that he revered the LORD. But now his creditor is coming to take my two boys as his slaves."
>
> Elisha replied to her, "How can I help you? Tell me, what do you have in your house?"

"Your servant has nothing there at all," she said, "except a small jar of olive oil."

Elisha said, "Go around and ask all your neighbors for empty jars. Don't ask for just a few. Then go inside and shut the door behind you and your sons. Pour oil into all the jars, and as each is filled, put it to one side."

She left him and shut the door behind her and her sons. They brought the jars to her and she kept pouring. When all the jars were full, she said to her son, "Bring me another one."

But he replied, "There is not a jar left." Then the oil stopped flowing.

She went and told the man of God, and he said, "Go, sell the oil and pay your debts. You and your sons can live on what is left."

This story is interesting because it shows a few key elements of God's faithfulness. First, it shows a generational blessing: the husband had revered the Lord, so his widow and sons reaped the benefits of his obedience. Secondly, the widow had to use what she had on hand, and she also reached out to others for help. Similarly, we have to use the gifts and talents we have been given. At the same time, we should be willing to lean on or borrow the talents and abilities of others. Third, the widow had to operate in faith. She had no idea how this plan was going to work, but she trusted God's prophet and did as he asked. And finally, God filled every one of the containers that she was able to gather. He would have filled more containers, if she had any more to fill. He provided enough for her to pay all her debts and for her and her sons to live on the remainder. This is a clear sign that God blesses those who are *prepared* for the increase.

Deuteronomy 7:7,8 says,

> The LORD did not set his heart on you and choose you because you were more numerous than other nations, for you were the smallest of all nations! Rather, it was simply that the LORD loves you, and he was keeping the oath he had sworn to your ancestors. That is why the LORD rescued you with such a strong hand from your slavery and from the oppressive hand of Pharaoh, king of Egypt.

God reminds us that it is not by our ability or strength, but God in our smallness and need chose us and loved us. He exalts us and makes us strong. He brings us out of our oppression. When we are doing better, sometimes God reminds us that it's not because of us, but because of Him.

God has to tweak the hearts of His people constantly, because He understands their heart drift. The more we tend to focus on things other than God's divine purpose and plan, the more we fail to use those things for His glory.

Deuteronomy 10:16 says, "Therefore, change your hearts and stop being stubborn." Deuteronomy 10:21,22 says, "He alone is your God, the only one who is worthy of your praise, the one who has done these mighty miracles that you have seen with your own eyes. When your ancestors went down into Egypt, there were only seventy of them. But now the LORD your God has made you as numerous as the stars in the sky!" God multiplied them even in the midst of their bondage. When they went down into Egypt, there were only seventy of them, but now they were as numerous as the stars. In other words, according to the promise that God made to Abraham in Genesis 15-17, they looked like what God had declared.

Your vision can happen, too. Maybe you feel as if you're in a season of bondage and financial difficulty, but God is saying, "I'm bringing you out according to My word. You will come out better than when you went in. You will come out multiplied. You will come out stronger than you were when you went in, just like My people."

That is why God reminds His people that He alone is worthy of praise. He alone brought the people out of Egypt with mighty miracles. Deuteronomy 10:16 says, "Therefore, change your hearts and stop being stubborn." God will deal with the indifference in our lives and the contrariness in our hearts. But if we keep our hearts tender to Him, He can continue blessing us in a mighty way.

Deuteronomy 11:1-4 says,

> You must love the LORD your God and obey all his requirements, decrees, regulations, and commands. Keep in mind that I am not talking now to your children, who have never experienced the discipline of the LORD your God or seen his greatness and his strong hand and powerful arm. They didn't see the miraculous signs and wonders he performed in Egypt against Pharaoh and all his land. They didn't see what the LORD did to the armies of Egypt and to their horses and chariots—how he drowned them in the Red Sea as they were chasing you. He destroyed them, and they have not recovered to this very day!

I believe God wants to strike a blow to your enemies that they will never recover from. If we will trust God, He will strike a blow against debt and lack and fear and discouragement. It will be such an attack that our enemies will never recover. The instructions that the Lord gave can be summed up in this manner: love because you are loved. Respond because God has acted for you, and treasure God's Word in your heart because God has treasured you in His heart. No matter where you go, or how difficult things get, keep the Word alive in your heart because God is keeping you alive in His. You're always on His mind.

We sing a very popular song now, "You Are Not Forgotten." It declares over and over again that God knows your name and you are not forgotten. The reminder of that truth encourages us all. He remembers you in the covenant of His love. That's why there are so many references to the word "remember" in Scripture. I love word studies, and I love that particular word—*remember*—because it means to be joined or connected once again. When God tells us to remember His covenant and to remember the Lord your God, He is telling us to be rejoined and reconnected to the knowledge of His love and grace.

Dr. Mike Murdock talks about four tools that God gives us to help protect our peace. No matter where you find yourself, no matter what position life puts you in, you can maintain your peace because of these truths. Never allow upheaval or chaos to disinherit you from the blessings of God. The children of Israel had a deep-seated faith and trust that the God who had brought them into the land and through great struggles, would continue to support them. If you know that God is your source, then your heart will be filled with peace and trust in Him.

I love the way Hebrews 4:11 KJV puts it: "Let us labor to enter into the rest." (paraphrased). Speaking of the labor of faith, it is not something that we deserve on our own or earn by our works. Rest and peace are a result of laboring in faith, and that means casting down doubt and fear and hanging onto faith in the midst of very negative circumstances.

Here are the four principles from Dr. Murdock that will help you protect your peace:

1. Conflict leads to distraction from your vision

You get a bill in the mail you weren't expecting to receive. Conflict is introduced into the equation. It represents the trap of distraction. It causes you to lose your focus, to get your eyes off Jesus. Jesus refused to operate outside the arena of peace. Peace was a necessary atmosphere for Jesus' power to work, and peace is a necessary atmosphere for your life and for your continued success. So realize that conflict leads to the trap of distraction, and distraction is a luxury that you cannot afford.

2. You determine your own focus.

That is your choice. No one besides you can make you lose your focus. Focus creates feelings. What you focus on long enough will create the emotions that you desire. So many who have fear concerning their future have been like Peter, who focused on the waves, the evidence of the storm, rather than the stabilizing force in the storm, Christ Jesus. When Christ is our primary focus, Christ becomes our peace, as the Scripture says. Focus creates the feeling that you desire.

3. Pay any price to protect your focus.

In Mark 9, Jesus said that if your hand offends, you should cut it off. In other words, what distracts you? Whatever it is, you ought to cut it off. Obviously, this is not a literal cutting off of your hand but cutting off those things that might contaminate your faith and steal your focus from Him. Isaiah 26:3 says, "You will keep in perfect peace all who trust in you, all whose thoughts are fixed on you!" Whatever your mind is focused on and attached to, there your emotions will be as well, whether they are emotions of peace and rest, or emotions of chaos and upheaval.

4. The Holy Spirit produces love.

Romans 5:5 KJV says, "…the love of God is shed abroad in our hearts by the Holy Ghost which is given unto us." The love of God for us is that sense of security that we all need. First John 4:18 KJV says, "There is no fear in love; but perfect love casteth out fear: because fear hath torment. He that feareth is not made perfect in love." I used to wonder what the relationship was between fear and love and exactly what this Scripture was addressing. But then I realized that fear really speaks to our insecurity. Here the writer is saying that perfect love casts out fear, meaning insecurity. The perfect trust and understanding of how much God loves you removes every hint of insecurity. We used to say: "I've got a feeling everything is going to be all right." That is a faith declaration. Everything is going to be all right, because I understand that the love of God is on my life, is in my life, and is over my life. Because I am uniquely loved by Him, there is no way I can fail and no way I can lose. There is no way I can fall, because I am winning through His love.

I hope you will take these things and use them to protect your peace on a daily basis. There are plenty of distractions trying to steal our joy and peace, but we need to stay focused on the Lord. It reminds me of the story of the little 4-year-old who answered a knock at the door. The person asked, "Is your mom in?" The little child said, "No, she's in emotions right now."

"Emotions?" the person asked.

"No, I meant devotions," the child responded. Your devotion—your focus—regulates your emotions. When your devotion is in the right place, your emotions will be in the right place too. Keep the devotion strong. Keep your peace strong in the kingdom.

5

Fishing for Answers to Life and Family

———————◆◆◆———————

A Word from the Lord will stabilize the atmosphere in your life.

There is a great deal of financial pressure on families today. Many people have had to deal with tremendous stress. Stress is the fourth leading cause of cardiovascular disease. It plays a major role in family and marital problems as well. A *Newsweek* article recently said that over six million men were being treated for clinical depression—and that was just the number that they knew about. Our society is living in a pressure cooker of stress, and stress causes people to do strange things.

It's like the old joke about the old farmer whose wife had passed away after being kicked by an old mule. Their marriage was not the greatest; it was widely known that they had a pretty rocky relationship. At the funeral, as the farmer was standing at the head of the casket, women would come by and give a casual greeting and walk on, but some people noticed that as each man walked by, he would lean over and whisper something in the farmer's ear. There was some type of exchange between the old farmer and the men as they came to pay their last respects. Afterwards, a family member mentioned that he noticed that all the men came by and spent a longer time at the casket than the women did. He asked what exactly the men said. The old farmer replied that all the men wanted to know if the mule was for sale!

When people are going through difficult times, they often look for an easy way out. In this particular chapter, I am going to tell a lot of fish stories to help illustrate how we can win at life and win at family. I know the men are going to enjoy this chapter, and I hope the women can endure it!

Being prosperous is more than just having money in the bank or just making ends meet. Being prosperous is a state of the soul. The Word teaches us in 3 John 2 KJV, "Beloved, I wish above all things that thou mayest prosper and be in health, even as thy soul prospereth." In order to prosper in our souls, we have to have character. Character allows us to be "capacious" individuals—that is, people who have the *capacity* to contain a great deal, the capacity to have great lives and families, to contain a great deal of blessing and favor and financial wealth. We have to be people of integrity in order to have the capacity to succeed in every area of our lives.

I want to use an incredible passage of Scripture to illustrate the concept of fishing for answers to life and family. It is found in 1 Samuel 30. In 1 Samuel 30:1-2 it says, "Three days later, when David and his men arrived home at their town of Ziklag, they found that the Amalekites had made a raid into the Negev and Ziklag; they had crushed Ziklag and burned it to the ground. They had carried off the women and children and everyone else but without killing anyone."

What would happen if you arrived one day to find the enemy had your family and had damaged your household and your relationship with your wife and children?

The Bible teaches us that it profits us nothing to gain the whole world and lose our own souls. Similarly, it profits us nothing to gain a great deal of material wealth but lose our families in the process. We could talk about athletes or politicians or entrepreneurs. We could talk about Wall Street professionals and people in other professions who are not able to deal with the stress. They turn to drinking or drugs, or illicit relationships or infidelity, and in the process they lose it all. In particular, they lose the things that matter the most: family, love, children, and their future relationships. These things require the prosperity of an individual's *soul*.

In the course of making a living, many of us have discovered the sad reality that the American dream is slipping away. Many people wake up one day and realize that their families are distant, their relationships are all messed up, and they no longer recognize the person they are married to! They may have made some money, but they haven't made a great life. That is why Christ continues to focus us on the things that please God. When we put Him first, then all these other things will be added unto us. This is a perspective that every godly man ought to have.

So what do you do when you realize the enemy has your family? This happened to David. While he was out building new kingdoms and taking new territories, the enemy was at work in his family.

As men of God we cannot be oblivious. Our hearts must stay in tune with our spouses and our children. We are to "know the state of our flock." We need to know the condition of our families and be able to lead and encourage them. However, if we become too distant, we run the risk of being out of tune with them. That is true emptiness and true dissatisfaction.

When David saw the ruins, he realized what had happened to his family. We should pray for the spirit of discernment where our families are concerned. Sometimes we don't realize what is going on until we see the ruins, and the ruins for each of us are different. For some of you, your "ruin" takes the form of a distance in your relationship. You begin to experience disenchantment from your spouse. There is a lack of spirit, of zeal, of passion. You wake up and see the ruins of your children. They are drifting, becoming short with you and rude to you, not honoring you. You see the ruins of their own personal character and conduct—the friends they associate with, the things they do, and the words that come out of their mouth. All of a sudden you wake up and see the ruins, and you begin to realize the enemy has taken charge of your family.

On the television program called *While You Were Out*, homeowners take a mini vacation while a crew of designers and carpenters come in and remodel on a particular space in their house. They come home to a new reality, a better one. But so many times we are disconnected mentally and come home to a worse reality. While we are out fighting the battles that we think are important and focus on things that we think need our attention, the enemy is stealing the devotion of our children, and our spouses. We have to get reconnected to our reality and overcome the ominous cloud of darkness and depression that is looming over our homes.

The story of David restoring and recovering his family is a great example to the body of Christ. There are some great points here that we can use to recover and restore our own families. If you have some of the same character traits as David, then today, no matter what shape your life is in, you can draw hope from this book and recover the one thing that should matter the most, your family. With these traits, you will prosper in your soul, in your relationship with your wife, and in your relationship with your children. Ultimately, you will be called a prosperous individual.

1 Samuel 30:4 says that when David came upon the ruins and realized what had happened to his family, he wept until he could weep no more. This indicates that this event moved him emotionally. I see so many men today who are numb to their surroundings. It's as if they have been taken captive and hauled away, and they don't even realize it. Verse 4 says David was attacked from every side, but this event moved David and got his attention. His heart broke, and he began to weep, so there was still a part of him that was alive. There was a part of him that was still connected to reality. You have to stay connected to reality if you are going to recover and rescue your family. Don't pretend that everything is all right. Don't bury your head in Dish TV and pepperoni pizza and ignore reality. Get reconnected with the state of your household.

Change on the inside has to happen before change can happen on the outside. Self-appraisal is healthy and necessary for any child of God. Where am I? How am I doing relative to where I was? And for relationships: Are we improving? Are we getting stronger? How can I change to improve the situation? Every relationship, including your relationship with God, is strengthened when you study the person you are in relationship with and you evaluate yourself in that relationship. Then write your own personal appraisal of how you are doing in that relationship and what you are doing to build and make it stronger. So what if you don't win at business? So what if you don't win that sales award? Just don't make the mistake of wining at making money while losing on the home front.

FIRST TRAIT: RELIABILITY

I believe this points to trait number one, the trait of reliability. A reliable person is a person who can be counted on to do what is expected or required. They are loyal. They are level-headed. A reliable person will rise to the occasion and can be counted on in the tight spots and under pressure.

What is very interesting about this story, about David's battle with the Amalekites, is that David was fighting enemies that his elders never confronted. Maybe those who preceded David had the ability to eliminate the Amalekites, but they just put up with them. So many times we just put up with problems in relationships instead of slaying the enemy once and for all so that future generations don't have to. We fight enemies that our parents or grandparents should have confronted. But when you possess the trait of reliability, you rise above generational deficiency to say, "You can count on me. I will make a difference and change the situation."

Reliable people manage to stay free from the "bitter man" syndrome. You see people afflicted with this syndrome all the time. They are bitter, and they want everybody to know it. They have a chip on their shoulder. Somebody did them wrong, and now somebody is going to pay. We call this filtering. Some people still run their conversations and behavior through a filter of pain from something that happened several years ago. If we would confront and deal with our bitter man, we could have relationships that are functional, whole, healthy, and happy. That is what happens to so many marriages; they bog down in the pit of the bitter man syndrome.

David could have blamed others for his plight. He could have blamed his ancestors for not having dealt with the Amelekites. He could have looked outside of himself to solve his problems, but the first thing he did was allow his heart to melt. He allowed his heart to evaluate the situation properly.

I've been thinking about how this relates to a particular fishing trip I took many years ago. I learn a lot from fishing. You give a man a fishing pole, a beautiful body of water, a beautiful sunset, and a package of worms, and he is practically halfway to heaven. I have enjoyed my time fishing. I have enjoyed my time with my sons. I have enjoyed my time fellowshipping with others. And I have learned a great deal about life.

I went fishing with my good friend Robert Gonzales several years ago. This was after our family moved to the beautiful Rio Grande Valley. This trip would be my first exposure to saltwater fishing. Robert decided he would pay a guide to take us out fishing. It was a fall day and kind of cloudy. Our guide took off with us in this boat and headed towards a large bay. He began to bait the hooks and tell us that in a few minutes the tide would shift. It was almost as if he was a prophet. Behind us was an oyster reef, and he said that oyster reef would be exposed, creating a channel of water that would flow near us. The channel flow, he said, would bring with it a great deal of bait, and the larger fish would position themselves in a way that would enable them to pounce on the bait flowing with the channel.

Taking him at his word, we set up shop, baited our hooks, cast our lines and sat waiting. We waited and waited, and soon everything that he said would happen, began to happen just like he said it would. The tide changed, the oyster bar appeared, and the water began to flow. Five minutes later, our poles began to bend and we caught some beautiful red fish and trout that day, just by doing what he said. The guide was a reliable source. I was impressed that he knew that at this particular time, in this particular fishing hole, and with this particular bait, we could catch fish because it had happened like that in the past. He knew that the area had a track record. Our reliability should be like that fishing hole—regular, predictable, and seasonal, but consistently producing.

SECOND TRAIT: NOBILITY

The second trait is found in verse 7, where David makes a declaration as he begins to dry his tears. First Samuel 30:7-8 says: "Then he said to Abiathar the priest, 'Bring me the ephod!' So Abiathar brought it. Then David asked the LORD, 'Should I chase after this band of raiders? Will I catch them?' And the LORD told him, 'Yes, go after them. You will surely recover everything that was taken from you!'" It is awesome to know that the Lord has a fresh word for every season. You may be in a season of upheaval and chaos, but God has a word for your life that will bring stability to your situation.

This book, *Fearonomics*, is based on that. When the Lord spoke to me to write this book, He said, "Speak a word that will stabilize the spiritual atmosphere in people's lives." Sometimes when we receive a word from God, we think that magically, the next morning when we awake, everything is going to be just beautiful and in order. But when God speaks a word it is up to us to receive it, and there's a time period for that word to come to pass. The word also has a condition based on our response to it. David, in order to get his word, had to have a particular trait: nobility.

Noble means "famous or renowned, having a high moral quality and facing the facts with courage." Facing the facts with a heart of courage—not running, not fleeing, but facing up to a challenge. David had to get to a point where he could hear the Lord say that he would recover everything that was taken from him. Sometimes

116

all we hear is the voice of our pain. Sometimes all we hear is the voice of lack saying that there is no way. You can hear the enemy saying, "Hah! I've got you this time! Your back is up against a wall. You're in a corner. There is no way you're going to get out of this." It is hard for you to hear a word of recovery, a word of destiny, a word of restoration when you are in the toughest season of your life. You have to endure a few things in order to get that word.

Even as David was wiping tears from his eyes, his men were saying, "David, this is all your fault." He had bitter people in his life. He had people who wanted to attack and blame him. He had to get past their rejection. Similarly, you need to get past the feeling that you need to compare your life to the lives of others. These are unfair comparisons—how their families are doing or what they did to solve their problems. God has a unique word for your situation. You need to find that word because that is the only thing that is going to set you free.

In order to deal with the bitterness and the judgmental attitude of others, David had to have the trait of nobility. He had to look for the high moral ground. People who are noble don't settle for the low-lying areas where others are content to dwell. Others criticize and find fault. David overcame the complaining of his men. I love what it says in the latter part of verse 6: "But David found strength in the LORD his God." You find strength as you look to the Lord. What did David reach for? He reached for a place of ministry. He remembered the place of worship on an Israeli hillside where he enjoyed the presence of God.

The Bible says in verse 7 that he then found Abiathar, the priest. He found the man of God in his life. For many of you, it is time for you to go back to church. It is time for you to take on a new attitude. It is time for you to get back to Bible study. Look for solutions in the right places. The palm reader does not have the answer. Neither does your horoscope. You need to reach for a priestly anointing in your life just like David did. Get back to church; get to a place where you can receive spiritual accountability and hear a spiritual voice. David called for the ephod and put on a priestly garment. He put himself in the position of intercessor between God and the people. God wants us to put ourselves in a place of intercession between our families and Him. Put on your priestly garment. When you do, things will begin to shift and change in your life.

When some people find themselves in the tight spots of life, they tend to look for love in all the wrong places, just like the pop country song says. Their reaction to their circumstances varies depending on their pressure level and character level. David reached for the right thing in his time of crisis; he reached for the priestly robe. He turned to the Lord. He sought the Lord's face, and looked in the right direction for help. People who have the trait of nobility find the high moral ground and know where to find help in a time of crisis. They are able to face the facts with courage. When David heard the Lord say in 1 Samuel 30:8, "You will surely recover everything that was taken from you," he was able to press ahead. Those words gave him the courage to move forward. Sometimes individuals flee in a time of crisis. They run from trouble rather than facing it with courage and confidence.

Years ago my associate pastor, Carl, my son Christopher, and I were out on a fishing trip in a new area, the South Texas Gulf Coast. We saw what looked like a bunch of fish in the distance. One popular form of fishing is wade fishing, where you wade out to the fish, trying not to spook the fish or scare them away. Christopher was much smaller then; he was probably about 10 or 11 years old. We told him to stay with the boat and that we were going to go see what all the excitement was about. So we waded about the length of a football field. We were worn out. We arrived only to discover that bait fish were stirring up the water. They weren't game fish at all. While we were over there, about a hundred yards from the boat, Christopher had hooked a beautiful speckled trout. He held it up and shouted, "Is this what y'all are looking for?" I tell you, I felt as if I were two inches tall at that moment. He had a good laugh at our expense.

When I think about being people of nobility—and especially *men* of nobility—I think about how many times we go out looking for satisfaction, when if we had just stayed with the boat we could have found what we were looking for. If you will stay in your marriage, with your job, or in your church, you will find the very thing that you're seeking. It is important to stay with the boat. Some of the best fish are caught right there. Don't be distracted by other things that are splashing in the water around you when all the answers are right before you.

David did not have to go out looking for answers. He put on the priestly garment in the middle of his situation, right in the middle of ruin and disaster, the charred remains of his city, and the memory of his precious family. He put on his priestly garment, and began to seek the Lord. That is when the turnaround begins for you and me—when we seek the Lord in the middle of our crisis.

THIRD TRAIT: FLEXIBILITY

The third trait you need to rescue and recover your family is flexibility. *Flexibility* is defined as "the ability to bend without breaking." Do you have that trait today? Do you have that divine buoyancy, that ability to rebound? In basketball, it's so exciting to watch players score, but did you know that the majority of the points are scored on the rebound? Flexibility is the ability to recover after failure.

Continuing with David's story, 1 Samuel 30:11-19 says,

Along the way they found an Egyptian man in a field and brought him to David. They gave him some bread to eat and water to drink. They also gave him part of a fig cake and two clusters of raisins, for he hadn't had anything to eat or drink for three days and nights. Before long his strength returned.

"To whom do you belong, and where do you come from?" David asked him.

"I am an Egyptian—the slave of an Amalekite," he replied. "My master abandoned me three days ago because I was sick. We were on our way back from raiding the Kerethites in the Negev, the territory of Judah, and the land of Caleb, and we had just burned Ziklag."

"Will you lead me to this band of raiders?" David asked.

The young man replied, "If you take an oath in God's name that you will not kill me or give me back to my master, then I will guide you to them."

So he led David to them, and they found the Amalekites spread out across the fields, eating and drinking and dancing with joy because of the vast amount of plunder they had taken from the Philistines and the land of Judah. David and his men rushed in among them and slaughtered them throughout that night and the entire next day until evening. None of the Amalekites escaped except 400 young men who fled on camels. David got back everything the Amalekites had taken, and he rescued his two wives. Nothing was missing: small or great, son or daughter, nor anything else that had been taken. David brought everything back.

David and his men ministered to another's need, and God used that individual to minister to their need. One of your greatest gifts is the ability to give in time of famine. Learn to sow into others' lives. David could have said, "Man, I'm not going to help you. You don't know what I am going through." He could have said, "I just lost everything I had; I don't know where my family is. My house has been burned to the ground. I don't have time to help you." But on the contrary, he took time to minister to the man's need. God used that act of kindness to help David fulfill the word that God had given him.

God is able to locate your blessing for you. He will locate your deliverance. He can show you your provision in the midst of difficult times. God is able to speak to you as you journey along. He will give you direction and help you make sense out of your difficult season. This message of "finding your Egyptian" is so significant because there is an Egyptian in every one of our lives. God puts something or someone in our paths that is able to unlock understanding and enlightenment and take us to a greater place of blessing.

There is an incredible phenomenon in the region where we live, near a body of water called the lower Laguna Madre. I have not seen this particular phenomenon anywhere else in the world. It's called "following the birds." In this particular form of fishing, the red fish in this region, the red drum, feed off of the bottom of the bay, which is very shallow—sometimes only six inches to a foot deep. Half of their bodies are out of the water. When they begin to stir up the bait and the shrimp on the bottom, the sea gulls come and hover

over the red fish, sometimes even resting upon their backs. For a fisherman, that is like a red flag, a signal. What an incredible sight! When you see the birds hovering, you know that there are fish in the area. When you cast your line around the birds, you can almost be guaranteed a catch every time. It is an incredible phenomenon, an incredible sight, and a tremendous experience. It's called "fishing under the birds." I've caught beautiful trophy-sized fish under the birds. Follow the birds, and you will find the fish.

In God's economy, we are to follow His Spirit. Be on the alert for the Egyptian He has placed in your path. The Egyptian has the ability to take you to your place of blessing, to take you to your answer. God puts the birds in our path to help us—if we will study the signs and be flexible. David had to go out of his way to experience the blessing and get the word that he needed to find his direction.   He had to suspend his own agenda and help someone else in order to find his answer. In our lives, we sometimes need to suspend our agenda if we are going to experience God's provision and God's best for our lives. We have to put aside what we want to do and find God's will for the moment, for the hour.

Finding your Egyptian carries a second meaning as well. Finding the Egyptian slave or servant while we need direction from God speaks to our need to have a servant's heart. Our answers are connected to a willingness to serve God and do God's will. That servant's heart can become our deliverance, as we become flexible and adaptable to God's plan.

The Scripture in particular mentions the bondservant. The bondservant had a unique commitment to his master because he served out of loyalty and desire, not out of coercion. Often, a bondservant would fulfill his obligation but had such loyalty and love for his master that he willingly continued to serve. There are seven key traits to every bondservant. As you are becoming the servant God wants you to be, think about these seven traits.

1. The bondservant's time was no longer his own.

Can you sacrifice and forfeit your time and realize that your time is God's time? Are you willing to do whatever He desires for your life?

2. The bondservant studied to find new ways to serve the master.

Every circumstance in your life requires a unique way of dealing with it. You cannot address two situations in the same way. God will show you how to address every situation for your benefit and for your positive outcome.

3. Every bondservant built up the master's esteem.

That means he was a worshipper; he was devoted to his master's well-being. God rewards worshippers in tremendous ways. David was a worshipper. The fact that David reached for the priestly garment and sought a place of worship tells us that we ought to look for new ways to worship the Master. The key to unlocking the wisdom you need is in worship and building up the Master. When you build up the Master, you are built up as well.

4. The bondservant valued his master's thoughts and opinions.

Father knows best. Value God's thoughts and opinions, or you will miss your Egyptian. You'll miss the circumstance, the person, or the opportunity that is going to deliver you.

5. The bondservant made allowance for weakness.

Don't make excuses about why you can't do something. Instead, learn how to compensate and build strength to please the Master.

6. The bondservant quickly sought freedom from sin.

A bondservant quickly sought forgiveness from any transgression that he had committed against the Master. This is how we keep our hearts clear, how we learn to keep our lives free from worry and how we keep the lines of communication open so that we can hear from God at the right time.

7. The bondservant enjoyed serving in every way.

Somehow you have to find joy in the midst of your serving. When you find that joy, it will take you to your moment of deliverance. It will take you to your moment of breakthrough.

So far we have talked about three character traits every individual needs in order to rescue their family. We need to have these traits before we can help others. The first was reliability, the second was nobility, the third was flexibility, and finally, number four is endurance.

FOURTH TRAIT: ENDURANCE

Endurance is "the ability to hold up under pain or fatigue." The Bible says that when David and his men finally discovered where their families and their goods were, they began to fight. They had to fight through the night, all through the next day, and on until evening before they could recover everything that they had lost. The word of God was fulfilled; they recovered everything that had been taken, but they had to fight for it. They had to endure through the night and into the next day before they could see that word fulfilled.

How many of you are willing to endure the fight through the night and persevere through negative circumstances? How many fight the temptation to compromise your good ethics for short-term gratification? You have to be ready to endure through the night test of temptation.

When Joseph was in Potiphar's house and Potiphar's wife was tempting him, he had to endure a lengthy night season. He had to resist his flesh in order to receive in the spirit. There is night season in every one of us. There is a season where we face the temptation to be discouraged and to throw in the towel. David had to choose to remove himself from the group of discouraged people surrounding him. He had to be a beacon; he had to be a light for others. As the Scripture says, he found strength in the Lord. He went to a place in God where he found the strength to overcome his negative situation.

This particular point on endurance and holding up under pain and fatigue reminds me of yet another fishing story. They say that the two happiest days in the lives of boat owners are the day they buy the boat and the day they sell the boat. Everything in between is maintenance. In the bay system where we live, there are a lot of shallow waters and sandbars. You really have to know the area, and you have to know your equipment. One of the last times I took my boat out was not a happy experience.

My associate, my son, and I thought we would slip away for a quick little fishing trip. It turned into a disaster that lasted nearly four hours. We started out by getting the truck stuck at the ramp. We couldn't get the trailer back out of the water. We were stuck. A gentleman came to try to help us, and then he fell in the water, fully clothed. Eventually he swam over and tied a rope around my trailer and lifted it up to get it floating. We were then able to free the truck and get the trailer out. At that point, I was ready to go home. The gentleman said, "Well, you came this far. You might as well go fishing. Got the trailer unstuck, now there's nothing to worry about."

He convinced me, so we took off and went to the first little fishing hole. Pastor Carl caught a really nice red fish right away.

Things seemed to be looking up, but after a while the fish weren't biting any longer, so we decided to go to a new spot. Against my better judgment, I cut through an area that looked as if the water was deep enough, but suddenly the boat ran aground onto a sandbar. We could not move; we were thoroughly stuck. Even after much labor, frustration, and stress, we still could not move the boat. Finally, in the distance I saw a man in an air boat. I waved my hands so he would see us and, thank God, we got his attention. He had just pulled another boat off a sandbar. For a hundred dollars—the only money I had on me—he pulled the boat out of the mud to the safety of deeper waters. At that point I told my fishing buddies, "I think we are done for the day." Not long after that, I decided I would get out of boating.

So many people end up the way I did that day. They go through a series of negative circumstances, and after being stuck several times, they decide to give up, sell the boat, pull in the sails, and stop trying to stay afloat. I encourage you today that it does not matter how many times you've been stuck. It does not matter how many negative experiences you have had. Stay in the game, stay in the water, and stay afloat. Have the endurance to finish what you started.

David's story of recovering his family and being restored can be your story and can be your reality. Practice these traits. Ask God for these traits, and ask God to help you to recover what you have lost. If you arrive one day to realize that your family has been taken, then I pray that the Lord will help you recover those things that are most precious to you.

Mark Abraham gave me an article the other day about the movie *Flash of Genius. Flash of Genius* is inspired by the true story of Dr. Robert Kerns. After creating the intermittent windshield wiper,

Kerns pitched his idea to General Motors, Ford, and Chrysler. All three companies turned him down, only to steal his idea and add intermittent wipers to all their vehicles. Dr. Kerns decided to take on the Ford Motor company in a legal battle that no one believed he could win. He later challenged Chrysler, GM, and Mercedes as well.

Early on in the film, Dr. Kerns had not yet invented his famous windshield wiper. He was working as a mechanical engineering professor at Williams State University. As the scene opened, Dr. Kerns was writing the word "ethics" on a chalkboard. His students entered the classroom. He turned and said, "Morning, everybody. I want to welcome you all to the first day of the quarter for applied electrical engineering. My name is Dr. Kerns, and I would like to start by talking to you about ethics." I can't think of a job or a career where the understanding of ethics is more important than engineering. Dr. Kerns continues, "Who designed the artificial aortic heart valve? An engineer did that. Who designed the gas chambers at Auschwitz? An engineer did that too. One man was responsible for saving tens of thousands of lives. Another man helped kill millions. Now I don't know what any of you are going to end up doing in your lives, but I guarantee you that there will come a day when you have a decision to make. And it won't be as easy as deciding between a heart valve and a gas chamber." That's another powerful truth to illustrate that in the critical moments, in the defining moments, your character will lead you. I pray that your character, rather than convenience, will affect your decision. Convenience will lead to compromise, but character will lead to conquest. Keep fishing. You never know what you are going to catch.

We were at Disney World for Christmas, just as we had planned to be. We had looked forward to this great trip, to have Christmas at Disney World. Rides, amusement, fun, shows, hotdogs, popcorn, cotton candy—are you getting hungry? It was the trip of a lifetime. That night, all eyes were on the sky. We had to stop in the midst of a crowded street as thousands of people lifted their eyes to see what all the commotion was about. Although it was very crowded, the atmosphere was incredible as we stood shoulder-to-shoulder on the crowded street and lifted our heads skyward. We stopped to watch. What was it? In the air, a skywriter was writing messages. But not just any messages—they were messages of hope written in the sky. They were messages of God's love, of John 3:16, messages that Jesus saves. For a moment, our hearts drifted away from the rides and amusement to the writing in the sky; people of every nationality and from every country and speaking every language you can imagine, stood with us and focused on the messages in the sky. I thought about how quickly our focus can change when we look up.

We are surrounded by people we don't understand and people who don't understand us. We are surrounded by different situations, yet one message can unify the moment. One message can cut through the confusion and the crowd and bring a central hope and a central theme. That is what this book is about. God wrote a message to us thousands of years ago, saying that no matter how you might feel right now in the crowd, no matter how congested and confusing things are, don't look down. For a moment, let time be suspended. Look up and pay attention to the messages of hope from heaven.

6
EMPTY

---◆---

"Yes, a person is a fool to store up earthly wealth but not have a rich relationship with God."

Luke 12:21

The Word of God teaches us the right perspective to have concerning money and the acquiring of material possessions. Luke 12:15 says, "Then he said, 'Beware! Guard against every kind of greed. Life is not measured by how much you own.'" The King James rendering of this verse says that life does not consist of the things that a man possesses. The word *consist* is an incredible word in the Greek that means "to be." If you apply those two words, "to be," you understand what Christ was saying. He was talking about a person's identity: who you are is not what you own.

We live in a world of status symbols. People measure your identity by the label on your clothes, the car you drive, the neighborhood you live in, the people you associate with, and the clubs you belong to. We allow things and labels to define who we are. But Jesus reminds us that our identity is not measured by how much we own. You can't measure your life that way. When you do, you are setting yourself up for disappointment. You are setting yourself up for disaster.

Paul wrote in Colossians 1:15, "Christ is the visible image of the invisible God. He existed before anything was created and is supreme over all creation." Everything that we know, we know in Christ. Everything that was created was created by Him. He is supreme over all of creation. We should establish this truth in our lives in order to have right priorities and right judgment. We try to put bandages on our lives and fix our problems but fail to acknowledge God until everything is falling apart.

But you see, Jesus is the visible image of the invisible God. If you want to know what is pleasing to God, look to Christ. If you want to know what is complimentary to God, look to Christ. He is the visible image of the Father's pleasure. The Bible says that Jesus existed before anything was created and is supreme over all creation. Guess what? We are a part of this creation. Trying to fix your life and make things work on your own is trying to take the place of the Creator. Surely the God who created all things will cause our futures to have purpose if we'll just allow Him to apply His creative touch to our lives.

Colossians 1:16 says, "For through Him [that is, through Christ] God created everything in heavenly realms and on earth." He made the things we can see and the things we can't see. Everything was created through Him and for Him. Let's look at this a little bit closer. He made the things that we can see and the things we can't see. What things can we not see? We can't see the future; we can't see tomorrow. We don't know what is around the next bend, but He made those things. If we live our lives in union with Him, then He will cause us to master and overcome the things we can't control. He is reigning over the things that are out of our control.

This verse refers to the things that we cannot see, such as thrones, kingdoms, rulers, and authorities in the unseen world. We talk about authority, dominion, and power, which are given by God. He gives us these things so that we won't stress out over the future, over things we can't see, or things we can't fix. If understand that all these things are within Christ's reach, then we won't spend our time stressing over them. We will spend our time worshipping Him and giving Christ rightful place in our lives. The things we can't see are significant to God. You can't necessarily see a person's character, but our relationship with God anchors us. People talk about the iceberg concept. It is not the 10 percent that is above the water that matters; it is the 90 percent below the surface that sunk the Titanic. The portion that we can't see below the surface is the weightier matter, the more significant. We need to build our lives on that. Remember, the things we have do not define our lives. Our identities are not based on those things.

Colossians 1:17 says, "He existed before anything else, and he holds all creation together." Christ is also the head of His body, the Church. He is the beginning, supreme over all. He is first in everything. If we can just grasp that and make Him first in everything, then we won't have to worry about the stock market. We won't have to worry about the economy. Let's just be faithful to God and do what He tells us to do, and He will bless our activities.

In Luke 12:15 Jesus said that your life does not consist, or your identity does not come from, what you have. In Colossians 1:17, the word "consist" is used again, and it says "by Him all things consist." It means to "set or put together." Every life is set by God; every life that is submitted to God is put together by God.

If God puts your life together, then when you go through a series of negative circumstances your life won't fall apart. You won't lose your bearings. You won't run off and go crazy because He is the definition of your life. While we put emphasis on acquiring things and use labels to determine our worth, God looks at our hearts. He determines our worth by the contents of our hearts. If you have Him, then you may lose things, but you will always be restored. God will restore the things that were taken from your life.

Our emphasis should not be on building a big bank account but on building a rich relationship with God. I recently read an article in *Vanity Fair* magazine about the Bernie Madoff scandal that touched so many people. It really showed what happens when people base their identities in money rather than in a rich relationship with God. The article said:

> Madoff's fall hit Palm Beach like a hurricane. In the best restaurants, diners blanched after learning by cell phone that their money was gone. Shell-shocked guests were at the December 11 kickoff party for the International Red Cross ball in the home of Susan and Don Talesko, the U.S. distributor of Tommy Hilfiger, who looked as if they had just seen a ghost, said someone who was there. People came in and said, "Oh my God! I lost this much, that much. How much did he hit you for?" From the private clubs to the seaside mansions, a curse of almost Biblical proportions, as it came to be called, descended like an evil cloud. It spread like wildfire.

> Lawrence Lemer, author of *Madness under the Royal Palms*, told me about one of his early callers, a business titan, who had lost fifty million overnight. His charity was wiped out. His foundation was wiped out. The retirement for his employees was wiped out. Lemer got a frantic call from a woman who

was at the annual ball of a Jewish charity. She said it was like the Titanic going down. People were screaming and yelling. She had never seen such emotion, said Lemer. Everybody was drunk. People who don't drink drank like their lives were over. It wasn't just their money that Madoff stole from the Jews of Palm Beach; it was what their money enabled them to do. Palm Beach is a Jewish majority. Lemer said explaining, "over the years the resort had evolved from a bastion of wasp anti-Semitism, where Jews were not allowed in some of the hotels, much less the private clubs. In some cases they are still not in a town whose business and social arenas were dominated by Jews. They are richer than wasps," said Lemer. "They are basically more cultured and more generous. This is their island or was until December 11. This not only destroys them financially but also destroys a sense of superiority that they had."

Notice the writer mentioned a sense of superiority. Wealth can create a sense of superiority if it's not built the right way. This is not an anti-money or an anti-prosperity statement. We just need to place prosperity in its proper place so it does not rule you, but you rule it.

In the same article, Rabbi Moshe got it right. He invited his local congregation to look beyond money and financial losses to matters of deeper importance. The Word of the Lord says in Luke 12:21, "Yes, a person is a fool to store up earthly wealth but not have a rich relationship with God." We need to understand money's purpose: money is for your assignment. Money is given to you to finance what God calls you to do in this earth. It should never be your sole source. It is a necessary means to help you fulfill the purpose that God has for you.

Solomon, one of the wisest and wealthiest men who ever lived, gives us a clear understanding of what it means to have things but still feel empty and purposeless in life. In Ecclesiastes 2:1-7, Solomon said of the vast wealth that he had accumulated:

I said to myself, "Come on, let's try pleasure. Let's look for the 'good things' in life." But I found that this, too, was meaningless. So I said, "Laughter is silly. What good does it do to seek pleasure?" After much thought, I decided to cheer myself with wine. And while still seeking wisdom, I clutched at foolishness. In this way, I tried to experience the only happiness most people find during their brief life in this world.

I also tried to find meaning by building huge homes for myself and by planting beautiful vineyards. I made gardens and parks, filling them with all kinds of fruit trees. I built reservoirs to collect the water to irrigate my many flourishing groves. I bought slaves, both men and women, and others were born into my household. I also owned large herds and flocks, more than any of the kings who had lived in Jerusalem before me.

Solomon had accumulated a massive amount of wealth. In forty years, he had accumulated 172,000 talents of gold, numerous chariots, horses, ships, and servants—all these things gave him great influence. But notice the wording that comes up in Ecclesiastes 2:17, "Everything is meaningless—like chasing the wind." Just as so many people today are searching for identity, we come back to the Greek word *consist*, to be looking for identity, looking for something to build self-esteem or build pride. Yet Solomon said that all of these things left him feeling as if life was meaningless. Other translations use the term *empty*, like smoke that is here today and gone tomorrow. No lasting fulfillment or real inner peace remains.

When Solomon started his journey to wealth, he used a great inheritance from his father, David, as seed to get started. From the beginning, he started by seeking God's wisdom and building a life based on pleasing God. Many people veer from Godly wisdom. Instead they end up trusting the *things* that wisdom has built for them. In Ecclesiastes, Solomon looked back over his past mistakes and failures, realizing what he had built: a utopia of self-pleasure that no longer left him fulfilled.

Second Chronicles 1:12 says, "I will certainly give you the wisdom and knowledge you requested. But I will also give you wealth, riches, and fame such as no other king has had before you or will ever have in the future!" So Solomon received wealth, riches, and fame because he pursued wisdom. The problem was that when weightier matters of character and heart were left to chance, he was left empty. Many people today who have amassed a great deal of wealth are some of the most insecure people when it comes to life. That points to the symptom of misplaced identity.

I love the old saying: "when you are down to nothing, God is up to something." The believer always has that hint of faith. We can use examples like Solomon's life to say that we don't have to go down that road. We don't have to go from up to down. We don't have to go from trusting God to trusting things, but we can go from trusting God to trusting God. We can continue to see His blessing and His provision reign in our life because we keep our hearts in the right place.

There's an old joke about two gentlemen who had been flying a small single-engine plane that crashed near a deserted island. The two men survived and swam to shore.

After several days, provisions began to run out. One man reported to the other, "There are no provisions on the island. In a few days we are going to run out of food." The other man looked at him and said, "Don't worry; I make $250,000 a week."

The gentleman looked at him in astonishment and asked, "What difference does that make? You don't understand. I have been all over this island. There is limited provision. There is no fresh water. We are going to die."

His friend looked at him and said, "You don't understand. I make $250,000 a week."

By this time, the man was absolutely livid. He was beside himself. He shouted, "Have you lost your mind? That $250,000 a week is not going help you here! We have no food! We have no running water! We have no radio! We are doomed on this island!"

Then the man said one more time, "You don't understand. I make $250,000 a week, and I'm a tither. My pastor will find us."

Through the years the Lord has been faithful to my wife, Anne, and me. He has provided and come through for us. When it looks like there is no way, right at the brink of disaster, God always comes through.

Several years ago we were youth pastors at a church that hosted a monthly youth event called Saturday Night Life. Several churches from the city would come. It was well-attended—several hundred youth would join us every month.

During one of these events, we were responsible for raising funds for the budget. That night not very much came in—not even enough to cover the event. I had told the Lord earlier, "You have to provide for the event, or we can't continue to have it." The church had limited resources to give us for the event, so there was nowhere to turn but to the Lord. I will never forget what happened next. Midway through the service, I told my wife that when the band finished playing, I would tell everyone that this would probably be the last Saturday Night Life because we didn't have enough money to continue the event. Before I could get out of the foyer to head down to the front of the church, a couple approached me. They wanted to catch me before I went up front because they had something they wanted to hand me personally. This couple had just closed down a small mission across town, and they had decided to invest all the remaining resources in the youth event. They handed me their offering.

That night when the staff counted the offering, we had exactly the amount of money we needed to pay off the budget for that event. We were even able to pay for the next month and several months past that. It's amazing how good God is. When it looks as if there's not enough to continue, God always comes through in an incredible way. He will send provision into your life. That is the way the children of God ought to operate.

Solomon's heart was empty. He said his life was meaningless. He had all these things, everything we think of as important, yet his life was without meaning. Let's look at our pursuit of money and how people approach it in different ways. In an article in the April 2009 edition of *Men's Health* magazine, Richard Sine talked about four types of people: the guardian, the artisan, the idealist, and the rational individual. Maybe you can determine which one you are, and then we can look at the God-centered, God-motivated individual to see the attitude we ought to have toward money.

THE GUARDIAN

First, Sine talked about the guardian. If you are a guardian, money is a path to security for you and your family. You read financial planning books, save regularly, keep a budget, and are insured to the hilt. Your investments tend to be overly conservative. Well-educated guardians will tolerate risk for long-term benefit, says Greg Philbic, a finance professor at Penn State, who has assessed the risk inclinations of different temperaments. The current recession is hitting guardians the hardest, because, out of the four personality types, they've done the most to avoid financial distress.

If you're a guardian, a layoff makes you feel irresponsible. Debt makes you feel ashamed; you may feel as if you're spiraling toward depression. "Your way to beat money stress is to first vent a little," Sine says, "you've done a lot for your family and friends, and they won't mind indulging you." Next, let a financial expert chart a new course for you. Guardians like plans. They are the most likely of all the types to follow through, since sacrifice comes naturally to them.

THE ARTISAN

The next type Sine talked about is the artisan. For the artisan, money means a new plasma TV, World Series tickets, a Range Rover Sport, whatever you want now. "As an artisan, you see life as one big game," says Kim, "and a fat bank account proves you have won this round." Saving seems pointless, and traditional investing strategies are a total snooze. Of all the types, you are most prone to serious debt. When things go bad, you risk hitting auto-destruct by drinking, smoking, and eating yourself into oblivion.

THE IDEALIST

The next type Sine mentions is the idealist. Money is a stepping stone to your higher calling. Idealists are the healers, teachers, activists, and gurus of the world. You're on a ceaseless mission to improve yourself and the people who matter to you, and if someone pays you along the way, so much the better. But in caring for the world, you might forget to take care of yourself. Your apathy can leave you broke during retirement, and your generosity can push you into debt. You tend to be so optimistic that when things go bad financially, you might stay in denial.

THE RATIONAL

The fourth type is the rational. For the rational, money is proof of your superior brain power. People may find you cold, distant, or absent-minded, but since people aren't spreadsheets you have little use for them anyway. You may be as smart as you think. Rationals value and seek knowledge. Rationals choose risky investments because they look more at the up side when things turn south. They feel like failures. "A lot of those Wall Street geniuses whose elaborate risk models failed so spectacularly are probably rationals," says Sine. If you're a rational you are also prone to paralysis because you analyze and obsess over what went wrong and what could have gone wrong. Either way, you are standing when you should be running.

You may see a little bit of Solomon in all of four of these types—and maybe a little bit of yourself. No one type in particular stands out. As we look at this, we can learn from the Word of God how we should have the proper balance. We shouldn't necessarily be a rational who looks at money as evidence of superiority and strength from our brain power and our great intelligence. We shouldn't necessarily be an idealist, although we should help people and give and be mission driven. We also have to plan for the future. As artisans, we see a really materialistic view, getting all we can, but in the end if we haven't laid the proper foundation, all of our faith and trust will be in the things that we have. When those things are gone, faith and trust go too. As for the guardian, we need to be conservative, and we need to save; but we can't save to the point of becoming stingy and lacking generosity. We understand that it is our giving that continues to position us for a greater future in God—not holding on too tightly but learning to release everything lovingly into the hands of God. What are we building our lives out of? Are we building lives of substance? Are we building our lives from God's perspective? Are we building lives centered on greed?

We need to determine how much makes us happy. How much will it take to really satisfy you? A plasma TV in every room of your house? Do you need an indoor bowling alley, an Olympic-size swimming pool, a 10,000-square-foot mansion, a Starbucks inside your house, and a butler to serve you Skittles 24/7? Is that going to bring you happiness in life? Some people who have many possessions are the most miserable people on the planet, so we know that money by itself doesn't bring joy.

Jesus taught us to ask of Him so our joy may be full. God gives us things that bring lasting pleasure. His gifts fill our lives with contentment and peace.

There are things of greater significance in our lives than money— for instance, integrity. I once heard the story of an old Roman guard during the time of the twelve Caesars. Every day the guard would line up in parade formation. As the soldiers would go through their parade route, they would beat their breastplates. In unison these men would shout the Greek term *integretis*, which is where we get our word "integrity." They would beat their breasts and shout "integrity." That word was defined as material wholeness and completeness—not just of outward things but inward completeness and wholeness, and they would declare their integrity every day. History teaches us that as long as they stayed true to their integrity and wore their breastplate of righteousness, they won many battles and were a formidable opponent. But there came a time, under different leadership, when it was no longer necessary to march in parade formation and wear the breastplate. This piece of armor was no longer necessary. The men stopped shouting the word integrity. They stopped declaring and emphasizing integrity. That was the beginning of the Roman guard's demise. The same holds true for you and me today. When we part from our integrity, we begin the downward spiral toward oblivion.

Solomon was well-known. He was a strong man of influence. The Queen of Sheba and other dignitaries came just to look at the brilliance of the temple that Solomon built for God. Yet although he had great exposure and a high level of influence, he allowed his possessions to control his life and his heart instead of the pure wisdom of God that he had started out seeking.

In troubled times, more than any other time, God wants to make His children shine. He wants to make us examples of a positive nature to the world around us, positive examples of trust in what God can do even when people are in distress. When it seems as if resources are limited, God shows up in an abundant way.

Several years ago we built homes, lived in them for a year or two, and then sold them to make a little extra money to help send the kids through college. We built one particular house right at the beginning of the housing decline. Nobody in our neighborhood could sell their home. It was a very bad time for real estate sales. God had always favored Anne and me in everything we did to build and sell; God just had His hand on it. It was a beautiful home, and we had listed it in a pretty good price range. Nobody thought it would sell, but within two weeks, we had a buyer. It was a supernatural deal in a situation where it shouldn't have happened. Everybody thought it was impossible. God shone through in that moment.

Several months later, a local banker who lived just down the street from us called me in to his office. He asked, "How did you do it? I don't understand how you did it. My house has been on the market for a year and a half. How did you sell your house so quickly?" I remember with joy being able to tell him that God did it. That is the favor of God, and we give God all the glory. These are the kinds of things that should be happening frequently in our lives, to witness to the world and to those who don't understand God's economy. Our faith and trust in God, will bring us through adverse times. Your faith determines how you handle adversity.

News reports state that 71 percent of people suffer from stress as a result of the current economic crisis. One third suffer from serious stress. Stress can cause health problems and causes many people to break down and seek counseling. At the height of Fanny Mae's problems, one of its executives committed suicide —as if the organization's troubles hadn't been enough, he had personally lost a million dollars in investments. All around us we see despair and people giving up.

Back in the fall of 2008, my accountant came in from the church's school and said the school had fallen behind by about fifty or sixty thousand dollars. We needed a miracle. My first thought was where the money was going to come from. We prayed and gave it to the Lord, and the Lord reminded me of a familiar passage of Scripture in the book of Habakkuk that has always comforted me. The voice of the prophet Habakkuk cries out of this little-known Old Testament book. In Habakkuk 3:17-18, he says,

> Even though the fig trees have no blossoms,
> and there are no grapes on the vines;
> even though the olive crop fails,
> and the fields lie empty and barren;
> even though the flocks die in the fields,
> and the cattle barns are empty,
> yet I will rejoice in the LORD!
> I will be joyful in the God of my salvation!

Habakkuk 3:19 goes on to say, "The Sovereign LORD is my strength! He makes me as surefooted as a deer, able to tread upon the heights." What an incredible passage! Even in the midst of adversity Habakkuk chose to rejoice in the Lord. This is a great example for us.

What was Habakkuk going through personally? He was a young prophet of his time, relevant for his age. He would have been in tune with what was going on. The king at that time was Josiah, who began his reign at about age sixteen. Somewhere between age sixteen and twenty, he purged Jerusalem of all its idolatry. He overturned idols and ran the strange gods out of town and came against idol worship. He established that Jehovah was God and the Israelites would serve Him alone. That order had to come from somewhere. Order authority had to be re-established. Josiah began to do this. Somewhere in the process, Helkiah, a High Priest, discovered a copy of the Law from Deuteronomy. In it, they discovered God's call for their nation and also how they were to live. That is the way that life comes at us sometimes. We try to do our own thing and build our own utopia, do our best financially, and in the process God's will is revealed to us. God's knowledge comes to us, there is a change in our lives, and we redirect the way we live.

They also discovered the list of blessings and curses that Deuteronomy talks about in chapter 28. They realized that if they lived outside of God's Law and plan, they would be subject to all the curses in Deuteronomy. This terrified Josiah. At that time, no one could remember a time when they had lived within the Law. They had drifted that far. But the rediscovery of the Law helped them understand that it was only through continued obedience that they would see continued blessings in their life.

King Josiah got radical. He had the people tear down all the altars to the strange gods and build new altars to Jehovah. In time, Habakkuk saw that even though the king had commanded the people to worship a certain way, that didn't mean that they had changed their hearts. Knowing the Law did not produce holiness or right relationship with God. They knew the Law. Now they had discovered God's purpose, but many of them were living it out of obligation, not out of fresh response or revelation. It concerned Habakkuk greatly that the people had just changed altars and were worshipping Jehovah, but they were not worshiping from the heart. They were merely worshipping Him from necessity.

It is important that we worship God long-term, not just as a 9-1-1 God who we call on in times of need. He is consistent in every season, and we should be consistent in every season too. The Word adds hope to our lives. It adds the strength and determination to hold on through difficult times.

I heard a story about an experiment. A scientist put a rat in water in a dark room to see how long it could tread water in the darkness. In the dark room, the rat could only tread water for about three minutes. Then he took another rat and did the same thing, but in this room he put a light bulb in the corner. This rat was able to tread water and stay alive for more than thirty-six hours because he looked to the light—he had something to focus on. That is a powerful example for us. We need to look for the positives.

Habakkuk said, "Yet will I rejoice." There has to be a "yet" in your life that keeps you anchored to hope. We hear stories of individuals who have given up on life and committed suicide. A recent victim was in his early forties. Because of financial pressure, he cashed in. There was no light in his room to look to, but we have a light bulb on. If you focus on the light and have a "yet I will rejoice" attitude in your spirit, God will miraculously turn your situation around.

Habakkuk experienced great discouragement. He said things like this, in Habakkuk 1:2: "How long, O Lord, must I call for help? But you do not listen!" He felt as if God could not hear him. We have all felt at times as if God was a million miles away, yet He is as near as our next breath. Just because circumstances make us feel as if we are separated from hope, it doesn't mean we are. Praise God, we are never separated from hope! We are never alone. God is always with us.

Years ago I heard a story about a newspaper editor who had a dream to sail from America to Europe in a single-person craft. He wasn't well-known. He was an obscure, small-town newspaper editor, but he and his wife believed that he could fulfill his dream. So he went. It was an arduous trip. He suffered from dehydration. Many times he felt like giving up. He was tired of eating raw fish.

His mind began to play tricks on him, and he began to think, *This is all in vain. There is nobody to celebrate with me. Nobody is going to even know I have accomplished this if I make it to the other side of the ocean. Nobody cares about me.* But somehow he was able to find the resolve to hold on, finish his journey, and fulfill his dream.

As he approached England, his planned destination, he saw that the whole harbor was lined with ships that began to sound their horns. Cheering fans waved from the docks as his small craft floated into the harbor. The telegraph lines had been hot, and the news had gone on ahead of him. The news of what he was doing had beaten him to his destination, and he was greeted with cheering shouts upon his arrival. This speaks to us today: if we will stay faithful, if we will stay with the ship, that word will go ahead of us, and God will bring much-needed encouragement at the right time. Your accomplishments will be celebrated—but you have to find the joy inside you.

Habakkuk had to wrestle with a stubborn and rebellious people. They worshiped because they were forced to, not out of passion or genuine love for God. Habakkuk lived in the midst of that revolt. I think many times of what the apostle Paul said in Acts 26:2 KJV; it's a truth that can be applied to this situation. He said, "I think myself happy, king Agrippa." Any child of God has a capacity to think himself happy. What you meditate on, you will become over time. If you feed your mind on depression, you will become more depressed. If you feed your mind on joy and victory and the goodness of God, regardless of the circumstances, you will experience the joy of the Lord. The encouragement of the Lord will eventually light your soul.

Habakkuk 2:4 says, "The righteous will live by their faithfulness to God." He was instructing the people to be faithful to God. Stay faithful to God no matter how you feel; don't just serve God out of convenience. Don't be an occasional believer; be a committed believer.

Habakkuk called for revival in Habakkuk 3:2 NIV when he said, "LORD, I have heard of your fame; I stand in awe of your deeds, O LORD. Renew them in our day, in our time make them known; in wrath remember mercy." He asked for God to do something in his day to reach his generation. Habakkuk was able to set his sights above all the negatives around him. He understood that because of the people's activities, famine and distress were overtaking the land.

If you will remember, Habakkuk 3:17-18 says, "Even though the fig trees have no blossoms, and there are no grapes on the vines; even though the olive crop fails, and the fields lie empty and barren; even though the flocks die in the fields, and the cattle barns are empty, yet I will rejoice in the LORD!" As he was penning these words to God, he looked up on a high cliff and God gave him a visual for his sermon. There he saw a mountain goat, sure-footed despite the danger of the heights. The mountain goat was just a step away from disaster, scaling an incredible rock cliff, and it reminded Habakkuk that even though believers walk on the heights, only a step away from disaster, they walk by faith. God is able help His people to be sure-footed in their time of trouble.

For many of you, it is time to set new goals. Your old goals have changed because of changing circumstances. Allow the Holy Spirit to work on a new goal in you. We went through a campaign here at Livingway called "Beyond the Walls." It first started out in 2004 and 2005. We had a big banner we put on the wall that read "Beyond the Walls in 2005." We had planned to expand our church and double our seating capacity. It didn't happen that year, so we changed the year on the sign. We just kept changing the year: "Beyond the Walls in 2005," "Beyond the Walls in 2006." Some of you just need to change the calendar year, but don't lose the vision. Now we sit in a beautiful new expansion that cost almost three quarter of a million dollars—paid for—because God is faithful. It would have been easy for me to tear the banner down and say, "That was an embarrassment—that is never going to happen." But God wants us to stay faithful to the dream, and He will support us in it.

Many Scriptures echo what verse 18 says, "Yet will I rejoice." In Psalm 42:5 NIV, the psalmist said, "for I will yet praise him." Psalm 43:5 NIV also says, "for I will yet praise him." Psalm 45:17 says, "I will bring honor to your name in every generation. Therefore, the nations will praise you forever and ever." That represents a continued commitment to praise God in everything. Praise is a weapon. I know you my not feel like praising Him, but if you will get the spirit of "yet I will rejoice," God will make you sure-footed like that mountain goat. You may be steps away from disaster, but He has promised that you will not fall or falter in your pursuit.

In 1 Peter 4:12, Peter writes, "Dear friends, don't be surprised at the fiery trials you are going through." We cannot be taken by surprise. We live in a hostile world. Problems are everywhere, and everybody has to deal with them. But God has made a way for His children. He always has a way of escape. No matter what your situation is today, choose to be like Habakkuk; choose to find the positive. Choose to rejoice in God, and your praise will sustain you through the storm.

Pastor Bob Moorehead wrote a commitment statement that might encourage you: "I am a part of the fellowship of the unashamed. The die has been cast. The decision has been made. I have stepped over the line. I will not look back, let up, slow down, back away, or be still. My past is redeemed. My present makes sense. My future is secure. I am finished and done with low living, slight walking, small planning, smooth knees, colorless dreams, tamed visions, mundane talking, cheap giving, and dwarfed goals. I no longer need preeminence, prosperity, position, promotions, plaudits, or popularity. I don't have to be right, first, tops, recognized, praised, regarded, or rewarded. I now live by faith, lean on His presence, love with patience, live by prayer, and labor with power. My face is set, my gait is fast, my goal is heaven, my road is narrow, my way is rough, my companions are few, my guide is reliable, and my mission is clear. I cannot be bought, compromised, deterred, lured away, turned back, deluded, or delayed. I will not flinch in the face of sacrifice, hesitate in the presence of adversity, negotiate at the table of the enemy, ponder at the pool of popularity, or meander in the maze of mediocrity. I won't give up, shut up, let up, slow up until I have stayed up, stored up, prayed up, paid up, and spoken up for the cause of Christ. I am a disciple of Christ. I must go until He comes. Give until I drop. Preach to all I know. And work till He stops me. And when Jesus comes for His own, He will not have any trouble recognizing me. My banner is clear. I am a part of the fellowship of the unashamed."

7

MAD MONEY

But Moses told the people, "Don't be afraid. Just stand still and watch the Lord rescue you today. The Egyptians you see today will never be seen again. The Lord himself will fight for you. Just stay calm."

Exodus 14:13-14

It's not at all audacious to believe God for His abundance in your life. We serve an incredible God, a great God who created the heavens and the earth and all that is. It is nothing for our God the Creator to provide for our small needs and to do so in an extravagant way. Experts say that we don't have a clue as to what people's limits are; all the tests, stopwatches, and finish lines in the world can't measure human potential. The only limit we have is our ability to dream beyond our circumstances. Our dreams - however big, however small - are the only limits in our lives.

The truth is that God wants to prosper you. I heard an old joke about a titled Irish man who said that when he died he wanted to take all of his assets with him. He wanted all of his money to be buried with him. Everybody knew his wish. So at his funeral his wife waited almost to the last minute, and right before they shut the casket she walked abruptly up to it and shoved something inside. When she got back to her seat, her friend asked, "You didn't do it, did you—you didn't put all his worldly possessions in the casket with him?" She said, "Yes, he said he wanted to take it with him when he went." The friend said, "I can't believe you did that!" "Oh, don't worry about it," the wife said. "I wrote him a check. He won't be able to cash it up there."

Although we can't take our worldly positions with us, God wants us to be supplied well in this life. The enemy is not happy when you are successful. Your enemy Satan wants to do everything he can to fight your prosperity and your blessing. When you are blessed, you are a threat to the enemy's kingdom. When you are successful, you have the ability to bless and help others. You can spread the gospel to reach people who have never even heard the gospel. It takes funds to do that. It takes resources to reach people for Christ.

The enemy's primary attack is against your finances so that he can minimize the reach of God's kingdom. When I started studying the topic of Mad Money—not the television show, a newspaper article, or a sitcom—I discovered what the Word teaches in Exodus 14. Exodus is where Israel broke out of bondage from Pharaoh's tyrannical rule. It is a day of freedom. In the midst of celebrating that victory, Exodus 14:5-7 says, "When word reached the king of Egypt that the Israelites had fled, Pharaoh and his officials changed their minds. 'What have we done, letting all those Israelite slaves get away?' they asked. So Pharaoh harnessed his chariot and called up his troops. He took with him 600 of Egypt's best chariots, along with the rest of the chariots of Egypt, each with its commander." Pharaoh had realized the wealth that had been taken from him. He didn't just go after the people; he went after the money. He went after the resources that these slaves were taking with them out of bondage. Just like for the Israelites, when God brings us out, He brings us out in abundance. We come out of financial debt, and God brings us into financial freedom. When that starts to happen, the enemy is upset about it.

Many of you are under financial attack. Understand that the enemy is mad about your money. He is mad about your advancement. He is mad about your success. He is coming for your money, and his efforts are not about you but about thwarting the kingdom of God. He knows that God has to get it *to* you before He can get it *through* you. So the devil pursues with vigor to destroy your prosperity, to destroy your raise, and to destroy advancement in your life. He wants to hinder you at every turn.

As the Israelites realized they were being pursued by the enemy, Moses rose up. It says in Exodus 14:13-14, "But Moses told the people, 'Don't be afraid. Just stand still and watch the LORD rescue you today. The Egyptians you see today will never be seen again. The LORD himself will fight for you. Just stay calm.'" The Egyptians represent the attack on your money. If you will take this to heart the Lord is telling you today He will fight for you, and you will not see Satan try to steal from you again. Praise God! If you make your stand and remain strong through this time, it is quite possible that you will never have to deal with this form of financial attack again. God is about to cause your enemies to flee from you as you allow the Word of God to stabilize your life.

Exodus 14:15-16 says, "Then the LORD said to Moses, 'Why are you crying out to me? Tell the people to get moving! Pick up your staff and raise your hand over the sea. Divide the water so the Israelites can walk through the middle of the sea on dry ground.'"

God gave a command to stop crying and to start moving. Those are great instructions for us in this 21st century: stop crying and start acting. Deuteronomy 28:12 says the Lord will "bless all the work of your hands." If your hands are idle, then God doesn't have anything to bless. But as you work and begin to act on the Word of God then the hand of God works through your hands and causes miracles to happen.

Remember all the "fear nots" from the previous chapters we have studied? In order to be ready for advancement, you have to deal with fear. Put fear in its place. Do not allow fear to get a grip on your heart. The Lord will rescue you. Stop crying and start moving. You may be unemployed, but do what you can do. Go out and wash a relative's or neighbor's car, or go mow some lawns. It's not about the money. Get your hands moving so that God has something to bless.

Think big when it comes to God, and learn to be OK with prosperity and abundance. An article in the April 1988 issue of *Christian Retailing* revealed that the average charismatic Christian in America spent a total of just $2.17 a week on everything Christian, including their offering. If $2.17 is all we see of God in our lives, that's how big we see God. You can imagine why some of us are receiving the pitiful return we are receiving. First, you need to understand that God wants you to prosper. Third John 2 KJV says, "Beloved, I wish above all things that thou mayest prosper and be in health, even as thy soul prospereth." Stop keeping God small, and stop pursuing small things. When you start to pursue larger things, you will see God work miraculously in your life.

Years ago, I was in video sales. I was young and aggressive, and I remember going after one of the largest hotel chains in the country. I may have been young and inexperienced, but I had confidence that if this hotel chain was going to buy from anybody, they were going to buy from me. I'll never forget going up to their corporate offices in San Antonio, Texas, and meeting with them. They had to be thinking the whole time, *I don't know what this kid is doing in this place.* But we found favor and ended up landing that deal. It was a lucrative deal for our company, but if I had not had the faith to go and approach these people—and I believe it was because of my faith in God—I would never have known the potential that was possible. Our God is a big God, and we don't need to be intimidated by anything or anybody.

As you read this book, ask yourself: *What are the issues I need to face in order to prove God is a big God in my life?* When you start walking in prosperity, you need to know that Satan will attack you. When you say that God is the source of your prosperity and believe that God wants you to do well, you will face persecution not only from the enemy but from other people. Not everybody wants to celebrate your success. Not everyone is excited to see you prosper.

Mark 10:28-31 says,

> Then Peter began to speak up. "We've given up everything to follow you," he said.
>
> "Yes," Jesus replied, "and I assure you that everyone who has given up house or brothers or sisters or mother or father or children or property, for my sake and for the Good News, will receive now in return a hundred times as many houses, brothers, sisters, mothers, children, and property—along with persecution. And in the world to come that person will have eternal life. But many who are the greatest now will be least important then, and those who seem least important now will be the greatest then."

Jesus declared openly that persecution would come as a result of a hundredfold return in your life. With prosperity comes persecution. With prosperity comes misunderstanding. Walk above the intimidation factor and realize above all else that it is the will of God for you to prosper. If you are not in line with that truth, then you won't experience God's prosperity and His abundance.

I know some may read this and think, *Well, this is just another book on prosperity.* But this book is very well-balanced in putting God first and centering your life around His values, and then all these things will be added unto you. Another step in this process is understanding that if you are not at home with prosperity, prosperity will not be at home with you.

Luke 7:36-50 reads:

One of the Pharisees asked Jesus to have dinner with him, so Jesus went to his home and sat down to eat. When a certain immoral woman from that city heard he was eating there, she brought a beautiful alabaster jar filled with expensive perfume. Then she knelt behind him at his feet, weeping. Her tears fell on his feet, and she wiped them off with her hair. Then she kept kissing his feet and putting perfume on them.

When the Pharisee who had invited him saw this, he said to himself, "If this man were a prophet, he would know what kind of woman is touching him. She's a sinner!"

Then Jesus answered his thoughts. "Simon," he said to the Pharisee, "I have something to say to you."

"Go ahead, Teacher," Simon replied.

Then Jesus told him this story: "A man loaned money to two people—500 pieces of silver to one and 50 pieces to the other. But neither of them could repay him, so he kindly forgave them both, canceling their debts. Who do you suppose loved him more after that?"

Simon answered, "I suppose the one for whom he canceled the larger debt."

"That's right," Jesus said. Then he turned to the woman and said to Simon, "Look at this woman kneeling here. When I entered your home, you didn't offer me water to wash the dust from my feet, but she has washed them with her tears and wiped them with her hair. You didn't greet me with a kiss, but from the time I first came in, she has not stopped kissing my feet. You neglected the courtesy of olive oil to anoint my head, but she has anointed my feet with rare perfume.

"I tell you, her sins—and they are many—have been forgiven, so she has shown me much love. But a person who is forgiven little shows only little love." Then Jesus said to the woman, "Your sins are forgiven."

The men at the table said among themselves, "Who is this man, that he goes around forgiving sins?"

And Jesus said to the woman, "Your faith has saved you; go in peace."

The woman had burst into a room where there was indifference, a room where she knew she would not be well-received. But she came with an expensive gift, and anointed Jesus with perfume. She was criticized-those who are only willing to do less will always criticize those who are willing to do more. You are always likely to be criticized by those who are willing to do less. They will persecute and speak disparaging words. But she pressed through the persecution and lifted her offering in the presence of the Master, and He graciously received it. If Jesus didn't expect us to bring our best then He would have omitted this story. Those who press through the resentful, persecuting crowd and offer their best to the Master will be rewarded.

Jesus helped the crowd to understand that this woman gave out of the richness of her heart, out of her rich love and her need for God. Other people won't have the same passion that you do. Don't expect others to have the same love for the Master either. But don't let others limit your offering because of their lack of passion. There are negative side effects when you're being blessed. One of these side effects is being persecuted for what you believe, being persecuted for the prosperity and the blessing of God. Jesus turned to these unwilling Pharisees and said, "You did not even do what was customary, which was to offer to wash my feet, but she has brought this expensive perfume and went above and beyond what is expected in giving her best for Me."

The woman experienced a great benefit—and the benefits far outweigh the negative side effects—because she brought a quality gift to Christ and offered it. Yes, she was persecuted. Yes, she was resisted, but she saw a part of Christ that nobody else saw. She received His forgiveness, His mercy pardoning her sins, and His eyes of love piercing her cold, sinful soul and renewing her spirit. She saw a view of Him that no one else saw, kneeling in the presence of the Master. That's what true worship and a generous heart will do—it will bring you to a place where you'll see God as no one else sees Him. There will be those who misunderstand you and those who miss out on the blessing, but I speak to those who are faithful to God. You may be standing alone but when you stay faithful to your calling, God will bless you and those around you because of your obedience to Him. The woman experienced the overflow blessing of Christ's love because she was willing to press through the resistance that was all around her.

Some people just try to do the very least they can do. There's a popular commercial that asks, "What can you get for a dollar?" We can't allow our attitude to become "What can I get for a dollar?" or, "What's the least I can do? I want the most for the least investment." We should always pour out the best for the Master because His heart pours out the best for us.

A dear lady attended our church years ago. Her husband wouldn't let her give to the church. He said the church was there just to take all the people's money and it didn't care about the people, but she knew differently. She had a view of God that was different from her husband's at that time. She had a little change from selling eggs on the side, and she would bring an envelope filled with coins and sneak it into the offering basket. These folks were basically hillbillies and lived in the woods in a little bitty shack. Years later, God turned things around in their lives. They had a brand-new home and new cars and money for the first time. All I could think about was that little woman who did the right thing by God. God never forgot her investment. Even though small and insignificant to others, her offering was significant to God.

God wants us to be the awe and the envy of the world. He wants us to be set apart in the world. He wants the world to come to the church for advice and for direction. Your prosperity will come when you're able to recognize God in your life and you're able to see Him and acknowledge Him. Prosperity through Christ doesn't make you more selfish. It makes you more God-honoring.

Just recently, a gentleman in our church came in on Sunday morning with a special seed for the ministry. We prayed with him and blessed him and asked God to prosper that seed. A few days later at the Wednesday night service, he came in and said, "Pastor, what normally occurs in our business in a week's time occurred in one day's time. I just want to give honor and glory to God and let you know that we're going to continue to sow seed because we understand the ground is rich, and God multiplies the seed that we sow." Some people are oblivious to the blessing, laws, and processes of God, while others learn to look for Him at every turn and interchange of life. God wants us to be the awe and the envy of the world.

Recently, our church developed a program to help teenagers who had failed their senior year of high school and couldn't pass their exit tests. These young people were just forgotten and left to earn small wages without a college degree. We had experienced a great deal of persecution in our community from local colleges and public schools, but eventually these same organizations asked us to host a program that would help these young people graduate. Now the public schools send struggling students to us to educate them and help them through to the next level. That's what it means to be the awe and the envy of the world. God can turn the tables and have the world come to you for advice, leadership, and counsel. The church ought to be a bright, shining beacon of hope and a symbol of prosperity today - not worn out, run down, decrepit, or in ill repair. God has called us to be the envy of the world.

We see this revealed in the Old Testament prophecy of Isaiah. Isaiah 60:1-3 says: "Arise, Jerusalem! Let your light shine for all to see. For the glory of the LORD rises to shine on you. Darkness as black as night covers all the nations of the earth, but the glory of the LORD rises and appears over you. All nations will come to your light; mighty kings will come to see your radiance." This represents the beacon of hope in our dark world. He said all nations would come to us. One translation says the heathen will come, those without God will be drawn to the light that they find among God's people. They'll be drawn to the radiance.

God tells us to rise out of the depravity that circumstances have placed us in. Arise! The *Amplified Bible* says in verse 1: "ARISE [from the depression and prostration in which circumstances have kept you—rise to a new life]!" Rise above it in your spirit. The prophet goes on in verses 5 and 6: "Your eyes will shine, and your heart will thrill with joy, for merchants from around the world will come to you. They will bring you the wealth of many lands. Vast caravans of camels will converge on you, the camels of Midian and Ephah. The people of Sheba will bring gold and frankincense and will come worshiping the LORD." When prosperity and blessings are upon your life, you should respond with worship. God wants us to be the envy of the world. God wants everyone to see that we're a blessed and prosperous group, because He's with us.

The topic of money and financial prosperity stirs people up more than anything else. Years ago I was teaching a Sunday school class about how to break the lack attack-how to break free from lack and believe God for abundance and how to call the abundance into your life. As I was preaching, a man was grumbling in the back row. He was making a scene, talking to people around him. I thought maybe he had a problem with the Word. When I finished the message, he made a beeline for me, pointed a finger, and said, "Sir, you are doomed for hell for preaching this message!" He began to condemn me and speak in a derogatory way about the Word I preached that day. It's amazing to me that the message of hope and prosperity could stir up so many devils. It just proves that the enemy doesn't want you to prosper. If he's fighting anything at all, he's fighting the knowledge of how blessed and prosperous God wants you to be. So in this chapter, I'm going to load you up with Scriptures that support the fact that God wants you to be blessed. We will expose the poverty mentality and replace it with the spirit of prosperity.

There was a preacher who saw a golf jacket in the pro shop that he really wanted. He'd been eyeballing it for a while. One day some extra money came into his hands, and he decided he would break down and buy that jacket. He felt bad about it, but he really wanted that jacket. So he bought the jacket, put it on and went out for his golf round. He played the worst golf he had ever played before. He was so convicted, he felt as if he had been wrong by to buy that jacket. He returned the jacket to the pro shop out of guilt.

Later that day as he was driving home, the Spirit of the Lord dealt with him and said, "Son, number one, I never speak through condemnation, and number two, don't blame Me for your bad golf game. You've never needed My help to play badly before."

Although that story is amusing, it reminds us that God is not the God of condemnation. He's not mad at us for having nice things, or wanting nice things. We just have to use those things to glorify God and bring honor to Him. You don't have to explain away the good things in your life. Give glory to God, and He will always give you more to give Him glory about.

You have to ask yourself, "Do I have a pride mentality, a poverty mentality, or a prosperity mentality?" Pride says, "I deserve more." Pride never gets enough because it is never satisfied. Pride is concerned with what others see and think. Poverty says, "Oh, I should feel guilty about this. What are others going to think? What are people going to say? There are people worse off than I am." Prosperity, however, reflects a heart filled with gratitude that says, "Thank you!" It's a heart that acknowledges the goodness of God rather than our ability to make things happen.

When someone says you have a nice house, pride would say, "We were going to build it bigger." Poverty would say, "Oh, it was a foreclosure—I got a good deal." Gratitude would say, "God blessed us, and we give Him the glory." Someone might get a new suit, and pride would say, "It's tailor-made." Poverty would say, "Oh, I got it at half price." Gratitude would say, "Thank you! The Lord blessed me with it." If they have a nice car, pride would say, "I've got three more just like it." Poverty would say, "Oh, it's a company car. It's really not mine." Gratitude would say, "Thank you! The Lord blessed me with it." We have to learn how to relate stories of God's blessings to others—not with a wrong attitude but with the right attitude because He promised to bless you and make you a blessing. How are we ever going to lead the way for others if we're not allowing ourselves to prosper?

The area where we live and pastor Livingway Family Church is, according to the fact sheets, the poorest county per capita in the United States. Right off, the enemy would say, "How can you write a book on prosperity?" My response to that is, "Why not? Why shouldn't we write a book on prosperity in the midst of a region where there is so much poverty and lack and poverty mentality? How else are we going to lift the region higher?"

God has blessed Anne and me. A couple of years ago, we went to a car dealership to buy another Chevrolet. Before we got out of the place, the owner had blessed us with a brand-new Lincoln Navigator. It caused a stir in the church because people were thinking, *Why should a preacher be driving such a nice car?* Most of them didn't realize that we didn't go to the dealership to buy that car, but God blessed us with it. It was a "perk" from the Lord. It was good in our area that is supposed to be dominated by poverty and lack to see that God wants to prosper His people. If I don't set the standard as the man of God, as the pastor, then what do the people look to? What is the standard? They need to know that God wants His people to be blessed, and God called us to lead by example. God is calling you to be a standard-bearer. He's calling you to lead by example, to lift the lid of limitation off your life, and to believe that God wants you to prosper and be in health and walk in abundance, even as your soul prospers.

In 1 Timothy 6:9,10 Paul told Timothy: "But people who long to be rich fall into temptation and are trapped by many foolish and harmful desires that plunge them into ruin and destruction. For the love of money is the root of all kinds of evil. And some people, craving money, have wandered from the true faith and pierced themselves with many sorrows." It all comes back to keeping our hearts in the right place. We don't covet what other people have. "Covet" means to set your heart upon those kinds of things, but we set our hearts upon God, and His heart for us is to be blessed. First Timothy 6:17 says, "Teach those who are rich in this world not to be proud and not to trust in their money, which is so unreliable. Their trust should be in God, who richly gives us all we need for our enjoyment." That doesn't sound like a God who is broke. That doesn't sound as if He's trying to deprive us of something. He gives richly for our enjoyment. He wants us to be blessed. He wants us to be blessed and to remember that especially in times of adversity.

The enemy is mad about your money, and he wants to shut you down. But remember, the heart of God is for you to richly enjoy life. First Timothy 6:18,19 says, "Tell them to use their money to do good. They should be rich in good works and generous to those in need, always being ready to share with others. By doing this they will be storing up their treasure as a good foundation for the future so that they may experience true life." Those who have a good understanding of prosperity know that their generosity lays a foundation for future blessings. They store up of their treasures to make a good foundation for their future. Think of it as making a deposit. Some day in the future you'll need to make a withdrawal and you'll have something to draw on. Heaven will have something for you because you stored up and sent blessings ahead.

People who don't understand prosperity and blessing think God is too small to be generous. That is the very thing that is holding them back. The seed is the strength of your breakthrough. If you can break greed and selfishness, you're qualified to receive the blessing and prosperity of God. Many times we are persecuted for the things that we have. I have heard people say, "If you were really concerned about others, you would sell that house and move into an apartment and give that money to the poor." That is fine if the Spirit of God tells me to do that. I would certainly do it. The point is: how big is your God? Isn't He big enough to provide the house *and* to provide the things that we need to do our assignment *and* to give us the resources to be able to take care of the poor *and* to reach out to those who haven't received the revelation of God's plan? I believe God is big enough to take care of all those needs. God is big enough to provide for all these needs and not make us ride around on a bicycle with one suit of clothes and live in a cardboard shack. God is big enough to provide for your own needs and to bless you so that you can help those who are not yet strong enough to stand on their own. We need to talk about the future we desire, and constantly declare it because our words give life to our dreams. Your words create a pathway for your destiny.

Years ago, just after we moved into our auditorium, something stirred in my spirit. I was up in front of the congregation and started talking about the future—about having a gym and a youth center and reaching out to the young people in the community. That was so far from our reality that it wasn't even funny. We did not have the funds, or the resources, and we didn't even have the people. Although we didn't have the means to do it, we did have the faith and vision. We began to speak about where we were going. We declared it.

About two Sundays after declaring the vision, a gentleman came up and said, "Pastor, the Lord told me to pay for the foundation for this new facility." It really surprised me because number one, I did not think anybody in the congregation would be able to do that, and number two, I was not prepared to move that quickly. We were just recovering from the last major building project. It took all we had just to build our first auditorium and launch our school at the same time. It was a major act of faith. After the man told me that I said, "Sir, please understand this is going to be quite expensive. We're probably looking in the neighborhood of $25,000 for the foundation." It wasn't a house or anything like that; it was going to be a commercial building. I was trying to be nice to him. He said, "Pastor, please don't insult me. If you will go get the plans, I am prepared to pour the foundation. I understand that it is going to be more than a house foundation."

God took us at our word, and I immediately went and drew up some plans. Within three weeks, we were digging ground and getting permits and pouring a foundation. That building represented a supernatural move of God and it was built debt-free. It took us a little over a year to build a beautiful "extreme" youth center and gym, a cafeteria, and eight thousand square feet with classrooms. We started by speaking the future we desired. We had no provision, no promise, no donor—just words.

You can frame your future. You can frame your world with your words. What do you need? Employ your words and your conversation.

Psalms talks about ordering your conversation. Let your words be complementary with Scriptures; they need to line up with God's Word. God will breathe His power on that. It will blow your mind when you start speaking God's vision instead of speaking what you see, speaking your smallness as opposed to His greatness. Let His greatness consume your life, your vision, and your conversation.

Out of the abundance of the heart the mouth speaks. (Matthew 12:34.) You need several Scriptures working in your heart about what the Bible says about prosperity so the words of your mouth will fall in line with what you know in your heart. Get comfortable with prosperity. I have taught that to my people many times. You may not be able to afford the new car, but you need to go down and sit in it. Soak in the new car smell and think about what it is going to be like when you get it. Do something to give you the image of where you are going. God talks about prosperity all the way back to Genesis. Here are some prosperity Scriptures to build your arsenal of faith and belief.

Let's start in *The Message* Bible, Genesis 1:22. God says, "Prosper." God commands the people to prosper. Fill the oceans, fill the air, and reproduce on the earth. Genesis 1:28 MSG says, "God blessed them: 'Prosper! Reproduce! Fill Earth! Take charge!'" God expects us to use our authority to prosper and establish His will in the earth. He blessed them to prosper.

In Genesis 9:1 MSG God said, "Prosper! Reproduce! Fill the Earth! Every living creature." God gave the Word and commanded It to prosper. He commanded the people to prosper; He has commanded you to prosper. Genesis 34:8 MSG says, "Settle down among us and make yourselves at home. Prosper among us."

In Genesis 41:52 MSG, Joseph says, "God has prospered me in the land of my sorrow." Do you believe God will increase you in the land of sorrow? Away from his parents' home, in the midst of the season of hardship, God prospered Joseph, and God will prosper you. It is His will. In Genesis 48:3 MSG, Jacob said to Joseph, "The Strong God appeared to me at Luz in the land of Canaan and blessed me. He said, 'I'm going to make you prosperous and numerous, turn you into a congregation of tribes; and I'll turn this land over to your children coming after you as a permanent inheritance.'" What are you hearing Him say? God spoke to Jacob and said He was going to make him prosperous and numerous. I hear God speaking that to you today: "I am going to make you prosperous and numerous."

This is the Word of the Lord in Leviticus 26:6 MSG: "I'll make sure you prosper, make sure you grow in numbers." Hallelujah! Numbers 6:26 MSG says, "God look you full in the face and make you prosper." I don't know why so many people fight the message that God wants you to do well when He says so much about it in His Word.

Deuteronomy 8:1 MSG says, "Keep and live out the entire commandment that I am telling you today so you will live and prosper and enter and own the land that GOD promised to your ancestors." Take that as a word from God that he wants you to go from renting to owning. God wants you to prosper, and He wants you to own the land, to take title deed of it. The only requirement He gave was to *keep*, which means "to guard, set in order, and live out" the entire commandment that you have received. Keep, guard, and value the Word of God. He promised He will prosper you, and make you an owner—not a borrower, not a leaser, but an owner.

God thinks in different terms than we do; we have to learn to think on His level. For instance, in the Old Testament, Haggai 2:7-9 says,

"I will shake all the nations, and the treasures of all the nations will be brought to this Temple. I will fill this place with glory, says the LORD of Heaven's Armies. The silver is mine, and the gold is mine, says the LORD of Heaven's Armies. The future glory of this Temple will be greater than its past glory, says the LORD of Heaven's Armies. And in this place I will bring peace. I, the LORD of Heaven's Armies, have spoken!"

It is incredible to know that God is in charge. He said there would be a shaking, and then He would bring all the treasures of the nations and gather them to His temple. He said He would fill the temple with glory. He reminds us that all the silver and gold belong to Him and that our latter glory will be greater than the former.

Notice that one of the first mentions of the word "glory" in the Bible is connected to material blessings—silver and gold. When God fills our lives with His presence and we live lives that are close to His glory, then material blessings are sure to follow. God is reminding us as His children that all the money belongs to Him. It is not on Wall Street; it is not subject to a one-world government or the one-world council of churches or the Euro dollar. The Lord said, "I am the God who has all the silver and all the gold." He reminds us that He is our source. He also reminds us that He never finishes on a low note but always on a high note. Even the Scripture declares in Ephesians that He is coming after a church without spot, wrinkle, or blemish: a glorious Church. (Ephesians 5:27.) There is that word again, *glorious*. That is a Church that is well supplied for. It has all its needs met. It has more than enough to preach the gospel all over the world and have millions left over. You can believe for a little bit and receive it, or you can believe for a lot and receive it, depending on what level of giving you want to reach.

The attitude that God honors is: "When I am blessed, what I can give?" Look at the level of giving where you can be. Look at what you will be able to give. In other words, don't ask God to give you a certain salary each year. Tell God how much you would like to give away to help others each year. That is a God-honoring prayer. That is a prayer that God can get involved in.

In Deuteronomy 28:8 the Lord speaks a covenant word to remind the people, "The LORD will guarantee a blessing on everything you do and will fill your storehouses with grain. The LORD your God will bless you in the land he is giving you." He guarantees a blessing on everything you do. Having the guarantee of man is one thing. Having the guarantee of the God of heavens is another thing entirely! God says, *I will guarantee this. I am backing it with Myself. I am guaranteeing a blessing on everything you do. I will fill your storehouses with grain.*

One time a man came to church and wanted us to give him some money. He said the Lord sent him from Florida. He did not have a plan or any savings. He did not prepare for the ministry trip. He informed me that Jesus said that when you go forth you should not take anything with you, and you shouldn't have savings and shouldn't have any provisions with you—just live on the fly and hope that things work out in the process.

But Christ was not anti-savings. He was not anti-abundance by any means. Christ taught us the principles of giving, but He also taught us principles of storing. He taught us in Matthew 25 about being good stewards, about bringing more to the master than what we started out with. These principles would not be in Scripture if Jesus was against having a plan and anti-storehouse. There are so many more Scriptures that support prosperity and the ability to bless others than there are about living paycheck to paycheck.

Deuteronomy 28:8 says, "I am going to fill your storehouses"—plural, not singular—"I am going to fill your storehouses with grain." For some of us, the problem is that we have not built storehouses adequate enough to house the measure of His blessings. Desiring less than He is capable of giving is an insult to the power and presence of God. What many of you need to do is develop some storehouses. What I teach our people in our church is to go open a checking account, even if it is with the minimum. God will begin to fill your storehouse. Out of that storehouse you can build a treasury that will bless the world. You can send missionaries around the world and send the gospel to the outermost parts of the earth, but if you don't have a storehouse, you are saying that you don't believe that God is big enough to fill it.

Recently I read an excerpt from an incredible book called *The Storehouse Principle* written by Al Jandal and Van Crouch. Ask yourself a couple questions. What can you see yourself doing? What can you see yourself having? You won't receive any more than that—I can tell you that for sure. *The Storehouse Principle* starts out with Psalm 33:7: "He gathers the waters of the sea together as a heap; He lays up the deep in storehouses" (NASB).

In the book, Pastor Jandal shared:

In the early 1980's I went out to lunch with a pastor friend. By this time we had sold the little house and the twelve acre plot of land for a good profit which allowed us move into a nicer home closer to the church. Because of our personal storehouse we were again able to pay for it with cash. The church was also continuing to grow and we were looking to move into new facilities soon because we needed more room. God was helping us to grow as we obeyed him.

If you have ever been to Texas you know that we are famous for Bar-B-Q restaurants. The one my friend and I had gone to for lunch was old and rustic with heavy wooden tables and a wooden floor. As we sat there and we talked about the things pastors talk about and he told me about one of the messages that he preached recently at his church.

"Al," he said, "Let me ask you something—when you think of wood what do you think of?"

The question really caught me off guard. What was he talking about? "I don't ever really think of wood," I answered.

"No. No. No. Listen. Let me ask you again another way. If you picture wood in your head what do you think of?"

Still a bit confused by what he was saying I looked around the room for a moment and my eyes fell on one of the tables nearby. "Oh, I don't know, how about a wooden table?"

"Ok, that is good, but think about this now. When God thinks about wood He would think of something like the Redwood Forest or the Amazon Jungle. God does not think small like we do. He thinks big." Then he went on before I could respond. "When you think about rock what do you think of?"

Again I looked around. I caught a view of the gravel in the parking lot outside. So I said, "I don't know, how about rocks on a driveway?"

"Ok," he accepted, "but when God thinks of rock, He thinks of something like the Rocky Mountains, the Himalayas, the Appalachians or the Andes because He is the God of abundance." Again he went on, "When you think of water what do you think of?"

Again I wanted to say "I don't think about water," but I knew he would not accept that answer. So I looked around the room again, "How about a glass of water?"

"Well, to know what God thinks when He thinks of water you would have to go to the oceans of the world, the Pacific, Atlantic, Indian and all of them rolled into one because our God is a God of more than enough."

With that picture in mind, I got excited. What he was saying was true. God did not do anything without creating more than He needed. He always had hundreds, thousands, millions of times more than He needed in reserves. Yet if He knew that He could create anything He wanted, why didn't He just create enough to get by for the moment and then create the rest when He needed it later? Think about this for a moment. He could have created just one planet for humanity, yet He created a universe with billions of solar systems, many of which hold planets of their own. Why did He need so many extras? To feed Adam and Eve, He created a whole planet of food. Why so much? Why didn't He just wait for the generations to come to allow more fruit-bearing plants to appear as needed? If Adam and Eve needed a drink, would they have needed much more than a stream? But God created enough water to cover 70 percent of the earth. Did He really need so much in reserves to take care of His children?

According to Psalm 50, God owns all the creatures of the forest and the cattle on a thousand hills. Since He can create more any time He wants, wouldn't the cattle on ten hills or even a hundred have been enough? Look for a moment at what Psalm 33:5-9 NIV says about God's creation:

The LORD loves righteousness and justice;
>   the earth is full of his unfailing love.
By the word of the LORD the heavens were made,
>   their starry host by the breath of his mouth.
He gathers the waters of the sea into jars;
>   he puts the deep into storehouses.
Let all the earth fear the LORD;
>   let all the people of the world revere him.
For he spoke, and it came to be;
>   he commanded, and it stood firm.

God created so much water that He needed to put some of it in the storehouses of the deep to hold it in reserve. Would He ever need all that water? The truth is probably not, because He could always make more. Then why make all that extra? It's because of the nature of God. I began to see that it was just His nature. He is a God of extras, a God of reserves, a God of storehouses. He always has more than He needs, no matter what happens, even in the finite sense of what is on the earth. He will never run out, and we will never run out of what we need. God does not have a scarcity mentality.

Let me give you an example of what I mean. There are a lot of people worried today that we will run out of fossil fuels to heat our homes and power our cars. If you look at the statistics, this is a reasonable concern. Yet at the same time, technologies are already being developed to replace those fuels with hydrogen or solar power. In other words, as humanity needs it, God will reveal to us new technologies to meet our needs until He is ready to come back for us.

Could Adam and Eve have imagined an earth that could hold more than six billion people? Yet somehow we are surviving, despite the desperate need in some areas of the world. If you were to take all of the wealth and food of the world and divide it up, everyone would have more than enough. Why? Because God created vast storehouses of extra abundance when He created the earth.

Abundance is God's nature. When we settle for anything less, we are violating what His heart desires for us. Jesus taught us that when blessing comes in your life it will come with persecution. He said that you would receive a hundredfold return on your investment in the kingdom of God, but it would come with persecution. People would misunderstand and call you materialistic. Be willing to look past that if you know you are destined to bless humanity.

This is what Andrae Crouch said years ago—the gospel is free, but the pipes cost money. Getting the gospel out and reaching the world takes money. God wants to bring those funds through the children of God. So don't be intimidated by persecution.

Kathryn Kuhlman was constantly attacked in her ministry by religious leaders and the media because of a personal mistake. She never reacted out of pride. She never took on a persecution complex. Although she had natural reason to do so, even when she stumbled, she regained her strength in a way that should teach us all. Her ministry had such a presence of God that even when she walked into the California studios, her presence could be felt. Despite the multitudes who were healed and saved in her services, no one left looking at Mrs. Kuhlman. God took her from glory to glory worldwide, despite persecution and attacks.

Learn how to survive a night in the lion's den. Learn how to survive the attack of the enemy. Understand the weapons that the Lord has given you. 2 Corinthians 10:3-6 says, "We are human, but we don't wage war as humans do. We use God's mighty weapons, not worldly weapons, to knock down the strongholds of human reasoning and to destroy false arguments. We destroy every proud obstacle that keeps people from knowing God. We capture their rebellious thoughts and teach them to obey Christ. And after you have become fully obedient, we will punish everyone who remains disobedient." God has given us His weapons to pull down the strongholds of the enemy. God is a God of abundance. When He thinks about wood, He does not think about the wood your desk is made from but the Redwood Forest. He thinks about all the incredible gigantic elements of creation. He doesn't think about a glass of water on your desk; He thinks about the awesome oceans. That is the level of His thoughts. We have to integrate our thoughts with His thoughts if we are going to receive even a portion of His nature and abundance. The way we survive the attacks upon our life and upon our finances—you *will* go through seasons of attacks—is to do what Second Corinthians says. That is to take the weapons you have been given and use them against the enemy. The Bible says in Ephesians 6:13, KJV "Wherefore take unto you the whole armour of God, that ye may be able to withstand in the evil day, and having done all, to stand."

In his book *How to Survive an Attack,* Roberts Liardon talks about this being one of the key weapons that God has given us. There are several words in the Scripture that denote action on your part. No matter how beaten up and drained you feel, if you understand the principles we discussed, your heart will be in position for action. *Strong's Concordance* indicates that the Greek interpretation for the word *take* is "strength." It describes the word from the root of another word implying the same strength as the thrust of a ram. This verse could be expressed like this: "gather a thrusting strength to yourself through the Word of God so you may be able to oppose an attack by overcoming and establishing yourself."

Liardon goes on to say, "Acquaint yourself with the Word of God." Out of all your armor—faith, truth, healing, deliverance, prosperity, salvation, joy, peace, and soundness—the only thing that wounds the enemy is the sword of the Spirit or the Word of God (Ephesians 6:14-17). The Word must be strong in you. It is your security. The anointing of God can help fix your problems, but the Word of God keeps them fixed. That is why Hebrews 10:35 KJV says, "Cast not away therefore your confidence, which hath great recompence of reward." The Word of God is your confidence. The Word is the Sword of the Spirit, and when that is used in Scripture, it is used with the English word *wield* attached to it, which means "to use with skill, to use on purpose, to use with a particular plan in mind." We draw the Word for specific situations. We use the Word to overcome the attacks of the enemy. If it is financial, then you need a financial word. If it is physical healing, then you need words on healing. If it is family, then you need a family word.

Liardon points out that weapon number two is praise. Ephesians 5:18,19 KJV says, "And be not drunk with wine, wherein is excess; but be filled with the Spirit; Speaking to yourselves in psalms and hymns and spiritual songs, singing and making melody in your heart to the Lord." Praise is our weapon. Worship comes against the attacks of the enemy. Paul and Silas survived their overnight attack with a song in the prison. They had praise, and that praise sustained them. Their praise eventually opened up the prison doors. Their sustained praise eventually brought them into liberty and freedom. Don't neglect the weapon of praise that God gave you to bring you through your midnight hour.

The last weapon that Liardon talks about in his book is prayer. James 5:16 KJV says: "Confess your faults one to another, and pray one for another, that ye may be healed. The effectual fervent prayer of a righteous man availeth much." Anne and I believe strongly in the power of agreed prayer. We have seen the strength of it over and over again in our lives, marriage, and ministry. It is seems as if every time we have a financial need, especially a need in the ministry, as soon as we come together in agreed prayer something dynamic, almost instantaneous, happens that causes the need to be met and the finances to rapidly appear. Perhaps this flows from 1 Peter 3:7 that instructs husbands and wives to dwell together so their prayers will not be hindered. When we are unified in prayer, the prayers are stronger and the answers seem to come faster. Your weapon of prayer is a great asset in your being able to overcome.

Paul said in Romans 8:26,27 KJV, "Likewise the Spirit also helpeth our infirmities: for we know not what we should pray for as we ought: but the Spirit itself maketh intercession for us with groanings which cannot be uttered. And he that searcheth the hearts knoweth what is the mind of the Spirit, because he maketh intercession for the saints according to the will of God." When you allow the Holy Spirit into your prayer life and you don't know what to say or how to pray, the Holy Spirit will help you to pray so that tremendous blessings come into your life.

Another great Scripture on prayer is 1 John 5. First John 5:14,15 says: "And we are confident that he hears us whenever we ask for anything that pleases him. And since we know he hears us when we make our requests, we also know that he will give us what we ask for." The NLT says, "Whenever we ask for anything that pleases Him." The *King James* says, "if we ask any thing according to His will." The things that please God are the things that are in His Word. He has already told us these things. His nature is the nature of abundance. If we can ever pray at the level where God operates, then that will be a day of tremendous breakthrough and blessing for us and for the kingdom of God. When we pray the things that please His heart, we know He hears us, and when we make our requests, we also know that He will give us what we ask for.

Thank God for confidence in your heart and in your mind as you go to Him in prayer. God is not slack concerning His promises, but He gives exceedingly and abundantly to the child of God who asks in accordance with His will. You might be going through an attack. You might be in your fiery furnace or having your overnight stay in the lion's den, but whatever you do, keep your heart anchored in the weapons that our God gave you. The Word is your weapon, worship is your weapon, and prayer is your weapon. With just these three weapons—and those aren't the only weapons you have—you should be able to confront any situation in your life and overcome any season of adversity.

That is why this chapter is called "Mad Money"—because you've got money, and the enemy is mad about it. Just like Pharaoh in the Old Testament, he is coming with a vengeance to try to steal your blessing and try to keep you from enjoying life. If he can't keep you from life, he wants to keep you from enjoying your life; but remember, the Scripture says God has richly given us all things to enjoy. Don't let the enemy take the joy out of it. Claim your prosperity; know that it is in agreement with the nature of God. You are not weird. You are not a freak of nature. It is all right to dream and desire and believe for the greatness of God, *and you will have it.*

8
THE PRINCIPLE OF MULTIPLICATION

You will be enriched in every way so that you can always be generous.

2 Corinthians 9:11

David Vanoy made this statement: "God has already put enough money in the pockets of Christians to do everything He expects His Church to accomplish." We have reached the point where we are no longer dealing with just overcoming fear and just getting by through tough times. Now we are taking a quantum leap into a whole new level of belief and living. In this principle of multiplication, I will start out with giving you several Scriptures to renew your mind. We have already established that our God is an abundant God. By nature, abundance is His heart. It is fitting and right that if He is a benevolent God, then He will share His abundance with you. One way we can multiply our lives is to multiply the seed that we sow. Through seed sowing, God makes it possible for our lives to multiply, increase, and take on His nature, the nature of abundance.

Genesis 1:22 says, "Then God blessed them, saying, 'Be fruitful and multiply. Let the fish fill the seas, and let the birds multiply on the earth.'" In Genesis, God revealed the nature of His heart, the nature of multiplication. From the Genesis account He taught us to "multiply"—not add, not basic increase, but multiply. He commanded us to be fruitful. The commanded blessing of God is on our lives. We should wake up every day and say, "Thank You, Lord, that You have commanded me to be fruitful and to multiply." God gave us the ability to do that with His Word. His Word carries with it the power to release the potential that lies on the inside of us.

In Genesis 17, we continue to lay this foundation. God spoke to Abraham, the father of faith and an example of what faith ought to be, in Genesis 17:2: "I will make a covenant with you, by which I will guarantee to give you countless descendants." The King James says, "and will multiply thee exceedingly." God spoke a direct word to Abraham, saying, "Because of your faith, because of your obedience, I will multiply you exceedingly." That is God's will toward us as well. He wants to benefit our lives so that we are a people who walk in His abundance. In Leviticus 26:9 NASB He said, "So I will turn toward you and make you fruitful and multiply you, and I will confirm My covenant with you." Again God declared increase over our lives, to multiply what we are a part of.

Now let's bring this over into the New Testament. In 2 Corinthians 9:10-11 Paul says, "For God is the one who provides seed for the farmer and then bread to eat. In the same way, he will provide and increase your resources and then produce a great harvest of generosity in you. Yes, you will be enriched in every way so that you can always be generous. And when we take your gifts to those who need them, they will thank God." Just as God provides seed for the farmer and bread to eat, in the same way God is going to provide the seed for us. Many times we are looking for the answer; we are looking for the harvest and not the seed. God wants us to look for the opportunity, a seed-sowing event that will bring the harvest in our lives. Are we sensitive to seed-sowing? Are we sensitive to the God-seeds in our lives? Because it is those God-seeds that release incredible harvest.

Notice that God says this assignment of seed will produce a great harvest of generosity in you when you act upon it. When you see how God provides the seed, it makes you want to share. It makes you want to give. It is a great joy to me when God brings blessings into my life, because my first reaction is, "Now I have something to give; I have something to invest in somebody else's life." I get to see that seed continue to multiply and grow. God put that desire in us, a harvest joy, to be able to see the seed produce. In verse 11, He says, "Yes, you will be enriched in every way so you can always be generous." Let's not forget our purpose. God placed us on the earth to fulfill a unique assignment, and the money and resources we have been given are to aid us in our assignment. As long as we keep those resources attached to our assignment, our lives will stay in proper perspective. Again He reminds us, "I've enriched you so you can always be generous"—we live out of the overflow, we are generous out of the blessings and the touch of God in our lives.

Dr. Phil Pringle wrote in his book, *Keys to Financial Excellence*, that Jesus focuses on the motive behind our giving. The only motive He condemns is when we seek to impress others with our giving. He doesn't condemn giving in order to reap a harvest. Some of us think we are very pious when we announce that we do not give to get; we just give to give. However, the Lord doesn't have a problem with giving in order to reap a harvest. In fact in Luke 6:38 NKJV He teaches this very principle to motivate us: "Give, and it will be given to you: good measure, pressed down, shaken together, and running over will be put into your bosom. For with the measure that you use, it will be measured back to you."

Matthew 6:1-2 says, "Watch out! Don't do your good deeds publicly, to be admired by others, for you will lose the reward from your Father in heaven. When you give to someone in need, don't do as the hypocrites do—blowing trumpets in the synagogues and streets to call attention to their acts of charity! I tell you the truth, they have received all the reward they will ever get." When we give just so that others will notice, we are not really sowing; we are just dropping seed out in the open for others to see. But you cannot see the seed that's been sown in soil. For it to grow, it must remain hidden. If the person who has sown seed keeps pulling it out for everyone to see, that seed will never grow. We will not reap a harvest from seed sown to gain people's admiration. Dr. Pringle says that when we sow the seed, we leave it alone. The power of God goes to work on it, just as the soil goes to work on a seed that is planted in the ground.

Whenever we host a building fund, or if I need to raise people's faith in the area of giving and receiving, I ask people who have been blessed to testify about it. Sometimes they are hesitant to tell others what they have given. I urge them to tell when and how much they gave so others are inspired. Without these testimonies, I know that the program will only be 50 percent successful. As people hear what happened to others, they increase their giving or are inspired to keep on going when they felt like giving up. There is tremendous power in testimony. Jesus told us there are times when we should let our good works shine before men so they will glorify God (Matthew 5:16). There is nothing wrong in announcing what we've given. That is just fearful superstition. Rather it is all about motivation. If we want to impress others with our giving, then that is all we will do. However, when our motivation is to inspire others to give because of our testimony, our seed remains sown in the ground, ready to grow and produce a great harvest.

Seed sown with the right motive can bring a harvest that shows that God is a God of abundance. He is a multiplier. He multiplied oil and meal in the Old Testament. He multiplied strength for the Israelite soldiers. He multiplied the loaves and fish. God is into multiplication.

In John 12, when Christ was speaking about His own death and preparing His disciples for the days ahead, He used the analogy of sowing seed and of that seed multiplying. John 12:23,24 says, "Jesus replied, 'Now the time has come for the Son of Man to enter into his glory. I tell you the truth, unless a kernel of wheat is planted in the soil and dies, it remains alone. But its death will produce many new kernels—a plentiful harvest of new lives.'" Jesus said His life would be a seed that was planted, and because of Him there would be a multiplied harvest of souls. A plentiful harvest is what the New Living Translation calls "a plentiful harvest of new lives." God has promised plentiful harvest for your life. A farmer sows seed according to the harvest he desires. A farmer never expects just one seed to come back from his investment. If a farmer reaped ten acres last year, he has to sow more seed this year if he expects a hundred-acre harvest. If you don't sow into more acres, you can't receive a greater harvest.

There are many people who have been sowing at the same level for five years and that is why their living is at the same level. If you want to increase your living, you have to increase your sowing. Let your sowing regulate and determine your level of harvest. Wishing or hoping things will get better won't accomplish anything, but sowing a seed of faith according to the desire of your return will produce a larger harvest than you have yet received.

Dr. Mike Murdock talks about this in his book *31 Reasons that People Do Not Receive a Financial Harvest*. What he writes is in line with this book, *Fearonomics*, because so many people have pulled back and lessened their giving because of difficult times. Many refuse to sow seed during times of crisis. He says crisis creates fear. Dr. Murdock writes: "It happened to me several years ago. Through a parade of personal and ministry tragedies, I suddenly faced bankruptcy. I owed many times more than what I owned. I did not know what to do. I prayed, fasted, and used every business principle I knew. The wall refused to budge. It was like a mountain of debt that nothing could shake. I became intimidated. I felt like a failure. Other ministries were flourishing and were building huge buildings, and I couldn't even pay my CPA $1,500 to get a financial statement to present to the bank for a loan. I met with successful businessmen who offered to lend me $250,000 if I paid them $50,000 immediately. I did not have $5,000 in cash to my name. During those times Satan really appeared overpowering. Sometimes it's hard to truly believe that your pain will ever pass. I couldn't think straight. I would sit numbly in various meetings around the table of negotiation. My mind was in shock; my heart lost its fight. I could not budge the wall of debt."

Sometimes during the battles of life you will be tempted to withdraw, become timid and passive. Satan is a bully. Bullies delight in shy, timid people. It is important that you develop a fighting spirit. It is very important to resist the devil and he will flee from you (James 4:7). You must run toward your Goliath. David did, but he did not come in his own strength against his enemy. He came in the name of the Lord. Crisis distorts every picture of prosperity, but crisis is the place of miracles. It is not the place to shrink back, quit, or hoard your sowing.

Why is crisis time an important season to sow?

1. Your sowing will birth expectation and hope.

2. Expectation is the only magnet that attracts the miracle provisions God promised.

"But without faith it is impossible to please him: for he that cometh to God must believe that he is, and that he is a rewarder of them that diligently seek him" (Hebrews 11:6 KJV). If you refuse to sow, you destroy your own ability to expect a miracle. A farmer can only expect a harvest after he has planted a seed. So your sowing is what births your expectation. Your expectations bring the hundredfold return Jesus promised. Nothing is going to change for you financially until you can unleash expectation within you. Your crisis actually magnifies the size of your seed in the eyes of God.

> Jesus sat down opposite the place where the offerings were put and watched the crowd putting their money into the temple treasury. Many rich people threw in large amounts. But a poor widow came and put in two very small copper coins, worth only a fraction of a penny.
>
> Calling his disciples to him, Jesus said, "I tell you the truth, this poor widow has put more into the treasury than all the others. They all gave out of their wealth; but she, out of her poverty, put in everything—all she had to live on."
>
> Mark 12:41-44 NIV

Dr. Murdock goes on to say of this story,

"She did not have very much money. She was poor but her financial crisis enlarged her seed in the eyes of God. She gave more than anyone else in His opinion because of her crisis. That is why it is important to plant seed when your back is against the wall and you have very little. Your seed will carry more weight influence and potential for increase than a much larger seed you will have later when you are doing quite well."

Thousands hoard during crisis, but it is the most unwise thing they could do. If you sow during times of famine, your seed will open the windows of heaven. God will pour out a blessing for you that you can hardly contain. Those are incredible words, but they are true. A crisis multiplies the influence of your seed. If you are going through tough times, you have an even bigger reason to sow and release what is in your hand to God so that He can multiply it.

Probably the most familiar story in Scripture concerning multiplication is in Luke 9:12-17. Jesus had been preaching and teaching all day long. The Scripture says,

> Late in the afternoon the twelve disciples came to him and said, "Send the crowds away to the nearby villages and farms, so they can find food and lodging for the night. There is nothing to eat here in this remote place."
>
> But Jesus said, "You feed them."
>
> "But we have only five loaves of bread and two fish," they answered. "Or are you expecting us to go and buy enough food for this whole crowd?" For there were about 5,000 men there.

Jesus replied, "Tell them to sit down in groups of about fifty each." So the people all sat down. Jesus took the five loaves and two fish, looked up toward heaven, and blessed them. Then, breaking the loaves into pieces, he kept giving the bread and fish to the disciples so they could distribute it to the people. They all ate as much as they wanted, and afterward, the disciples picked up twelve baskets of leftovers!

What a powerful story of Christ's love and ability to multiply what we give Him!

ORDER

This story illustrates a couple important points. First, Jesus told the crowd to sit down in groups of fifty. That shows God's preference for *order*. When we look at the universe, we can see that God is a God of order. The human body and the way it functions reflect the order of God. God made things to function in precise order. It is important to note that Christ established order before multiplication. If you will use this one truth and start setting things in order, God can bless and multiply you. Organize your finances. Your finances might be in chaos. Your bills are running rampant, and you don't know which end is up. You need to take the time, pray about it, and act as well. Take some time to set your life and your financial structure in order. We talked about establishing bank accounts, but you could also spend time talking to a financial adviser. Ask for insight into your personal situation because everyone's situation is different. Just like Jesus first set the crowd in order, He tells us to first set our houses in order.

RESPONSIBILITY

Secondly, Jesus gave the *disciples* the responsibility of multiplication. He asked what they had and told them to feed the people with what they already had. In other words, God has always placed enough within our reach to meet the need in our lives. As the disciples took the food that they had, they began to distribute it. Then those five loaves and two fish were multiplied in their hands. They could not find the bottom of the basket. Even though the need was great—there were five thousand men, plus the women and children—they began to sow into that situation. Even though your need may be great, remember—the Master multiplies the substance in your hand. It is in your hand that He will multiply it. Notice that it is in the hand of distribution—the hand of generosity, the giving hand—that multiplication occurs.

BLESSING

A third point is that something must be blessed before it can multiply. The food was blessed by Jesus and then multiplied in the hands of the disciples. We have to learn the power of *blessing*. I am honored when members of our congregation who have been blessed will ask us to come and pray over their car or ask us to pray over a house they were blessed with. It shows that they want Jesus' blessing on the things they have been given so they can see those things multiplied and used by God. If we expect God's blessings on our businesses, our finances, and our careers, then we must give these things to the Lord. Then we qualify for the blessing and the multiplication that follows.

God set these seed-sowing principles in Genesis. Genesis 1:11 says, "Then God said, 'Let the land sprout with vegetation—every sort of seed-bearing plant, and trees that grow seed-bearing fruit. These seeds will then produce the kinds of plants and trees from which they came.' And that is what happened." Praise God! I love the way that is said in Scripture. God said He initiated the seed-bearing fruit, and that is exactly what happened. Every seed reproduced after its kind; the plants and the trees produced according to their origins. From Genesis we can see that God said it is all about the seed. The seed would reproduce.

In every situation there is a seed: your job, your life, your family, and your career. How you plant the seed determines the measure of what you reproduce. We can always have hope and solutions because we always have a seed. God said that if you plant that seed, it will reproduce after its own kind. Because the blessing of the Lord is upon the seed that we give to Him, then God can cause that seed to multiply. A farmer never expects to receive one seed back. It multiplies—first the blade, then the ear, then the full corn in the ear. Even within the stalk it has the ability of multiplication. That is why we have to know not to look for the *need* but to look for the *seed* in every situation. What is God saying? What is God speaking to me? Where is the seed that I can plant that will release multiplication in my life because I always have more than enough in God?

Paul says in 1 Corinthians 3:21-23: "So don't boast about following a particular human leader. For everything belongs to you—whether Paul or Apollos or Peter, or the world, or life and death, or the present and the future. Everything belongs to you, and you belong to Christ, and Christ belongs to God." We should go about our lives knowing that God has given us all the things we need to fulfill our assignment. It all belongs to us through Christ. That's why Paul wrote that we are not subject to man for our provision or for our receiving. He said remember, it all belongs to you through the Lord.

God has given us a seed to plant, and that seed watered, nourished, and fertilized will produce a multiplied harvest in our lives. When you give to God and you plant a seed, imagine the beginning of a life-giving river—everything downstream is blessed. When you sow, you release the blessing, which causes multiplication in your life and the lives all around you.

Romans 11:16 KJV says, "For if the firstfruit be holy, the lump is also holy: and if the root be holy, so are the branches." As we put God first, this carries over into our tithing and our first-fruit giving. When we put God first in these areas, the blessing flows into every part of our lives—our children and their lives and activities, our jobs, our bodies, our families, and our relationships. Everything is affected, because if the first fruit is holy then the lump (or "mass") is also holy. The lump of our life is holy and set apart, because we honor God first. We give Him first place and cause everything else to be blessed.

Hebrews 7:6-7 says, "But Melchizedek, who was not a descendant of Levi, collected a tenth from Abraham. And Melchizedek placed a blessing upon Abraham, the one who had already received the promises of God. And without question, the person who has the power to give a blessing is greater than the one who is blessed." This is a simple Old Testament truth that says that the inferior, which is us, is blessed by the superior, which is God, when the inferior yields our seed to the superior. His superior ability comes on our inferior seed and causes it to be multiplied.

The One who has the power is the One who receives the tithe. God extends His superior blessing upon us, the inferior, as we are submitted to Him. Everything is submitted to Him: our finances, our careers, our futures, and our lives. Hebrews 7:7 says, "Without question, the person who has the power to give a blessing is greater than the one who is blessed."

The priests who collect tithes are men who die. Melchizedek is greater than they are because we are told that he lives on. In addition, we might even say that the Levites, the ones who collected the tithe, paid the tithe to Melchizedek when their ancestor, Abraham, paid a tithe to him. For although Levites were not born yet, the seed by which they came was in Abraham's body when Melchizedek collected the tithe from him.

This shows us that the downstream principle is at work because of Abraham's obedient offering to God. It even caused his unborn son to be blessed and come under covenant with God. What are you carrying in you right now because your act of obedience? The decisions you make will determine the kind of future your children have. I believe that with all my heart.

My son Ryan has a supernatural ability to play the guitar and minister to others. When I was his age, I played the guitar in church. One day, God spoke to me and told me to give a very beautiful guitar to another young man in our church who was just learning to play. So I sowed that seed. That was a sacrifice. It was a beautiful guitar, and I really loved it. In the last couple of years, though, I have seen how God has blessed all my children, not only in musical ability but also with musical equipment. Ryan has had guitars given to him. Supernatural things have happened in his life. I hadn't thought much about that guitar that I gave away many, many years ago, but the Lord said, "What you sow in obedience will live in your future, and your children will reap from that harvest."

This is an incredible truth. The daily seeds that we sow may not show a harvest in our lifetimes, but our children and our children's children will continue to reap the benefits of our obedience. The lesser is blessed by the greater, and because we, the lesser, have submitted to God's great power, the blessing continues to flow and increase continues to happen.

Pastor Phil Pringle illustrates this truth so beautifully in his book *Keys to Financial Excellence*. He says that some people stop getting anything out of church anymore. They are leaving the church because they are no longer getting fed. Sometimes when I am visiting churches, people tell me they are going to leave because the pastor doesn't bring the food of the Word. Often the problem is simply that these people have ceased tithing. Someone told them that they did not think that the church was spending its money properly. They may not like the spending shown in the annual report. They may have been having problems in their cash flow, so they stop giving until things improve. Gradually, however, they come to believe there is no spiritual food in the church for them. They get critical and judgmental about just about everything around them. Their hearts close off to the ministry God has given them.

The simplest messages can contain the deepest truths if we are open and eager to hear. If a person is a tither, then it is a law of Scripture that they will receive food in the house of God. God challenges us to put Him to the test. Malachi 3:10 says, "Bring all the tithes into the storehouse so there will be enough food in my Temple. If you do,' says the LORD of Heaven's Armies, 'I will open the windows of heaven for you. I will pour out a blessing so great you won't have enough room to take it in! Try it! Put me to the test!'" This is the only invitation in the entire Bible to put God to the test. The *Living Bible* says, "Try it! Let Me prove it to you." The *King James* says, "and prove me now herewith." The NIV says, "Test me in this." The NRSV says, "put me to the test." God says that if we bring all the tithes into the church, two things will happen: There will be food in His house—spiritual nourishment—and He will pour out such blessing that there will not be enough room to contain it. You will be unable to accommodate the blessing of God when He pours it out.

A middle-aged legal firm manager and his family became Christians in our church and after a while, decided to become members. When he was confronted with the challenge of tithing, he felt very uncomfortable with the entire idea. One of our pastors counseled him and suggested that he try it for three months, and if at the end of that time he experienced no recognizable benefits, then he should cease tithing. This seemed fair to the man. He began tithing. Immediately he received a hefty salary increase from his firm, a brand-new car, and other blessings that he could not help but relate to the fact that he had begun to tithe.

Once people experience the power of tithing, they will never go back to life as usual. I love the passage in Malachi 3:8 that asks, "Will a man rob God? Yet you rob me. But you ask, 'How do we rob you?' In tithes and offerings." God is not able to be violated by you and me, by us withholding our tithe. Surely we could not rob God. There is not a gun big enough to pull off that kind of heist.

Instead, we rob Him of the opportunity to pour out blessings and bring good things in our lives. We rob Him of that opportunity by withholding from Him what already belongs to Him. That word *window* in Malachi means a channel. It means a conduit, a vehicle; an avenue of blessing. It refers to the various ways that God will bless you and prosper you. God promised windows. He doesn't just have one window but many means of blessing your life. Don't just look to one area. Don't look at your job alone. Man may set your salary, but God determines your income. Ultimately your income is in the hands of God when you become a tither and a giver to the work of the Lord.

Tithing is really not giving; tithing is returning because you can't give what doesn't belong to you. The tithe is the Lord's. The rest is ours to keep or give as we choose. So when we tithe and return to God what's actually His, He promised to do certain things for us. He promised that He would make avenues and windows of blessing available to us that we would not normally see. He said that things would happen in our lives that we would not normally experience. These things are supernatural events. They are above and beyond what is normal or expected.

In his book *Life Management*, Gerald Redmond writes about the need to rekindle the tithe. He writes, "Positions of privilege are not guarantees of success." Charles Swindoll said during a radio broadcast, "The Israelites had secured a privileged position with God. We are well aware of the history and the contemporary outcome of the Israelites regarding this position. No people have soared higher nor sunk lower. No nation can record victories comparable to the Israelites. Conversely neither has any nation suffered such horrible defeat. They always seemed to do well with their privileges, but they always appeared blind and deaf and insensitive to their responsibilities." The church is a spiritual duplication of the Israelites. Lamentations 3:22-23 says, "The faithful love of the LORD never ends! His mercies never cease. Great is his faithfulness; his mercies begin afresh each morning." God has great faithfulness, an inexhaustible wealth of forgiveness, a divine provision of unfailing devotion, and a perpetual commitment to renewal. If we do not fulfill the conditions of the promises of God, the blessings of those promises cannot continue. We readily admit that we are undeserving of God's blessings, but we seem to ignore God's call to fulfill our responsibilities, and thus we abuse our positions of privilege.

Our Western culture refuses to acknowledge the idea of God's judgment. America believes itself to be a Christian nation, built on the foundations of freedom of speech, public assembly, the press, and yes, religion. Congress reportedly begins each session with prayer. Our money is stamped "In God We Trust." We must be a Christian nation. The question is, are we really? Could we be in bondage and not know it? Could we be like the Israelites? A heathen who spoke a language they could not understand ruled them. Why do we no longer mine our coal, copper, and ore? Why is there such a drastic cutback on our oil production? Why do steel mills no longer function? Why are farms disappearing and foreign corporations taking over as we approach a decade of drought? We use these commodities now more than ever. In reality, we are not deficient in any one of these natural resources. Yet America has become dependent on other nations. The reality of God's judgment is glossed over by such terms as inflation, trade deficits, budget deficits, and global economy.

Independent surveys of religious organizations indicate that no more than 5 percent is given annually to charities, including the church, and an average of only 20 percent of church members pay tithes. The most pointed chapter in the Bible on tithing is Malachi 3, which includes one of the most frequently quoted Scriptures: "For I am the LORD, I change not" (Malachi 3:6 KJV). Redmond says that when a person asks about a suggested fault, he has already indicated his guilt. Being a victim of a robbery is serious, but robbing God is an even more serious crime. In Malachi 3 God urges, return to Me, obviously someone had not kept the ordinances. He also charges, you have robbed Me, something was taken that didn't belong them. God then tells them, you are cursed because of your disobedience: the nation robbed both God and itself.

The parable of the talents indicates that God intended for our lives to multiply. He intended for us to take the things we were given and cause them to increase for the kingdom of God. That is what the Bible calls stewardship. What is in our hand isn't that significant, but when we give what is in our hand, it becomes magnificent. What is in our hand may be small, but what is in His hand is great. The only way to release what is in His hand is to release what is in our hand.

A golf club in my hand is not worth very much. It's actually worth a great deal of frustration and stress because that ball won't go where I want it to; but a golf club in Tiger Woods' hand is worth millions of dollars. A basketball in my hand is not worth a whole lot—maybe a few missed baskets—but that same basketball in the hand of a superstar like Tony Parker or Kobe Bryant becomes a tool worth millions of dollars. Our lives in our hands can be disastrous, but our lives in His hands become valuable and significant. Your seed in your hand may be small and lonely, but your seed in His hands becomes a force to be reckoned with.

God invests in our lives based on what we are responsible for and what we are willing to be responsible for. In the parable of the talents, different amounts were given to three different people. Five talents were invested with one man, two with another, and one talent with another. The owner left for an extended trip. The servant who received the five bags of silver invested the money and earned five more. The servant with two bags of silver earned two more. But the servant who received one bag of silver dug a hole in the ground and hid the master's money. After a long time, the master returned from his trip and called the servants to give an account of how they had used his money.

Matthew 25:19-25 says,

"After a long time their master returned from his trip and called them to give an account of how they had used his money. The servant to whom he had entrusted the five bags of silver came forward with five more and said, 'Master, you gave me five bags of silver to invest, and I have earned five more.'

"The master was full of praise. 'Well done, my good and faithful servant. You have been faithful in handling this small amount, so now I will give you many more responsibilities. Let's celebrate together!'

"The servant who had received the two bags of silver came forward and said, 'Master, you gave me two bags of silver to invest, and I have earned two more.'

"The master said, 'Well done, my good and faithful servant. You have been faithful in handling this small amount, so now I will give you many more responsibilities. Let's celebrate together!'

"Then the servant with the one bag of silver came and said, 'Master, I knew you were a harsh man, harvesting crops you didn't plant and gathering crops you didn't cultivate. I was afraid I would lose your money, so I hid it in the earth. Look, here is your money back.'"

Now in Matthew 25:26-29, it says,

"But the master replied, 'You wicked and lazy servant! If you knew I harvested crops I didn't plant and gathered crops I didn't cultivate, why didn't you deposit my money in the bank? At least I could have gotten some interest on it.'

"Then he ordered, 'Take the money from this servant, and give it to the one with the ten bags of silver. To those who use well what they are given, even more will be given, and they will have an abundance. But from those who do nothing, even what little they have will be taken away.'"

There should be no mistake as to what the heart of God is concerning finances, investments, and increase. For us to think for one minute or to preach that God is not interested in increase, that He is not interested in our producing more than we started with, we'd have to be in total staunch denial about what the Scripture says.

God rewards those who use their resources to bring dividends into the kingdom of God. The heart of the master is revealed in verse 26, when he says, "You wicked and lazy servant." He said, "Depart from me. I can't even stand to look at you." But to those who use well what they are given, even more will be given. They will have an abundance. Those who do nothing will have their small possessions taken away. God expects us to use what we have been given. In the midst of troubling economic times, God has promised abundance for those of us who will use well what we have been given. The commanded blessing of God is upon the working hand; He said He will bless the work of your hand.

Notice that the Master wasn't satisfied with just getting his money back. He didn't celebrate the conservative heart. He expected interest, an increase on his investment. Who is your master? The Bible says you cannot serve two masters. For the believer, our master is God. This is how the master looks upon our finances. These are the expectations of our Father God toward the things that we have been given.

What I have is not my own. What I have belongs to the Master, and what I have is not money alone. "Silver and gold have I none but such as I have give I to thee." (Acts 3:6.) God has given us talents, He has given us time, He has given us breath, and He has given us treasure. God has given us many things. What will the Master find when He comes to hear an account of the many things that He has given us? He expects us to turn it into more than it was when He gave it to us. The passage here is clear. Investing what we've been given causes what we have to increase and become greater for His glory. It multiplies when it is invested. Seed doesn't multiply in the barn; seed multiplies in the ground. Whatever you have is a gift from God, and when you invest it, it brings glory to Him. It brings increase in the kingdom of God.

God has promised to bless the work of our hands. But God said if we are irresponsible then what we have will be taken and given to someone who will treat it responsibly. I am a firm believer in being faithful in the little things. Being faithful with what you have will cause more to be given to you. When you multiply the assets of the Master, it pleases Him and He will want to invest more in your life.

It is just the same with your earthly children. Anne and I try to give our children the tools and resources that they need in order to do what God has called them to do. It is a joy to buy them these tools and invest in their lives. Knowing that they use them well for the kingdom causes us to want them to have more. We want to be able to give them more tools to spread the gospel.

That is the way the Father is toward us. Notice how the *New Living Translation* frames this. It says that when the master learned that one servant had doubled the five talents and the second servant had doubled two talents, he said, "Let's celebrate together." God celebrates our good investments. God celebrates our return. God celebrates our increase. He takes joy in the prosperity of His servants.

He loves to see us do well. How can the Church think that God wants us to take a vow of poverty and that He somehow enjoys seeing us suffer? Think about the Father's heart. Think about your heart as a parent and wanting to see your children do well. God's heart is like that toward us. He delights in our prosperity and well-being. It brings Him joy to see us do well.

God also expects us to have the heart of an entrepreneur. An entrepreneur is one who invests. An entrepreneur doesn't play it safe. When an entrepreneur can't see the Master or necessarily even hear His voice, he still knows what pleases His heart. The entrepreneur is faithful in the Master's absence just as if the Master was there with him. Christ promised He would return again. He left us some incredible assets on the earth and in our lives. Ecclesiastes 5:9 KJV says, "The profit of the earth is for all..." God is no respecter of persons. The profit of the earth is for all, but He wants us to have an entrepreneurial spirit to reap the blessings.

The term *entrepreneur* is a French military word that was once used to describe a particular type of commander who undertook risky ventures for strategic gains. That's the heart of the servant, to multiply risky ventures for strategic gains. Today the term refers to businesspeople who are action-oriented. They are not just thinkers; they are also doers. Entrepreneurs make a risky decision and act upon it. They have passion for profit. That is the heart of God today. Do you have the heart of the Master? A passion for profit, realizing it's not about you, but about bringing increase for Him? The more we increase for the Master, the more His kingdom can advance upon the earth. When you live with that as your highest priority, then God will make your raise match your giving. Instead of asking what raise am I going to get this year, ask what can I give away this year?

When our giving surpasses our living, then our living will rise to our giving, and that is good news!

Out of great risk came great profit, and the master was pleased. It was risky for the one steward who had been given five talents to invest, not knowing what the master wanted. It was risky for the one who had been given two talents as well. However, they were both celebrated by the master when the master returned. The one who simply paid the master back was not rewarded. He was scolded and judged for his lack of trust. The servant with the one talent had a bunker mentality: let's hoard it; let's protect it; let's hold on. Many people during seasons of economic stress have a "hold on" mentality. They won't give, and they won't invest. The problem is not that we can't invest—it's that they won't invest where God told them to.

In his book *Multiplication*, Pastor Tommy Barnett from Phoenix, Arizona, wrote about the twelve traits that Christian entrepreneurs must have:

1. The Master chooses servants who will expand His kingdom. God looks upon our hearts. He chooses servants who will expand His kingdom. Do you have a desire to expand the kingdom? Is your desire in the right place? Is your motive right? God will check your motive, and when your motive is in expanding the Master's kingdom, then God will support that particular venture.

2. The Lord invests in people instead of stuff. Be aggressive about blessing others. Become a mentor. Sow your life into other people.

3. The Master is willing to release control. Our God is incredibly excited about releasing control. He is excited about delegation. The Bible said "For the eyes of the LORD run to and fro throughout the whole earth, to shew himself strong in the behalf of them whose heart is perfect toward him" (2 Chronicles 16:9 KJV). He wants us to emerge from mediocrity and become a willing vessel that He can use.

4. The Lord makes His servants accountable. To be a real Christian leader, you must be accountable to people who have a broader perspective than you do. Listen to wisdom from your superiors and the people around you.

5. The Master is willing to take risks. We have to have the heart of an entrepreneur. We have to be willing to take risks to bring strategic gain for the kingdom of God.

6. The Lord gives resources for His servants to use, not for them to hide. What an incredible truth! Sometimes we say, "I am going to save up for a rainy day" when He gives us resources. He gives us those resources to invest and to multiply His kingdom.

7. A wise servant brings to the Lord an increase that pleases Him. If we are faithful stewards, according to the Bible, we are bringing the Lord increase. Our lives are multiplying, and we understand that He celebrates that increase.

8. The increase also brings joy and great blessing to the servants. What a blessing it is to succeed—the joy of fulfillment, the joy of advancement and achievement. God looks at us with joy and blessing as His creation. He gave us a sense of that on the seventh day. He gives us that sense of rest and fulfillment and accomplishment and satisfaction after creation. He has given us opportunity to work with our hands and labor and draw plans and build buildings, because He knows that it creates a level of joy in us when we accomplish things and achieve things.

9. A negative attitude towards God becomes a basis for misunderstanding in the kingdom. You can't develop a negative attitude toward the Master. The one servant had a bunker mentality—hold on to the end. That displeased the master. The servant had a negative attitude toward God. Those who have negative attitudes concerning God and finances are opening the door for disaster. Misunderstanding God's motives will keep the kingdom from having its full effect in our lives.

10. Servants unwilling to invest are called wicked and lazy by God. God is not into laziness. God wants us to be studious and diligent. He wants us to be consistent and to have a good work ethic. God can and will always bless people who have a good work ethic. He will bless that above skill and talent any day. God will bless diligence and excellence.

11. Servants who fail to use what the Lord gives them will lose it. We've all heard the old adage "use it or lose it." We have been given incredible gifts from God, and we need to value them. We need to value everything we've been given as a gift from Him.

12. Servants who invest wisely will experience abundance. Abundance is a promise from God. It brings joy to the heart of the Master when we multiply the gifts that He's given us. It brings joy to His heart when we use the seed He has given us.

In the book of Corinthians, Paul said that God gives seed to the sower and the bread to the eater (2 Corintians 9:10). One rendering says, "He gives seed to the sower so there might be bread for the eater." God put in our hand the seed that creates the bread for the harvest. Why did He give you a seed? So you would invest it. He did not put the seed in your hand so you would call it a harvest. He put the seed in your hand so you would invest it. That seed invested causes incredible dividends in the kingdom.

Remember Malachi 3:8-11? Tithes and offerings rebuke the devourer. Sow seed on purpose. Anne and I have seen many blessings because we are target seed-sowers. If we have a need in a particular area, we sow a seed and name that seed. I don't have to stand up and scream and yell at the top of my lungs to get the devil to go. According to the Bible, I need to plant a seed that has a purpose attached to it. Target your seed.

It is important to compartmentalize—this is my tithe, and this is my offering. The tithe has a particular task, and the offering has a particular task. The tithe is God's protection. It is His insurance, to protect you from liabilities, from the devourer, and from things that could destroy you. The offering has a particular assignment on it. It brings multiplication and increase—some thirtyfold, some sixtyfold, some a hundredfold return. Give your seed a specific assignment.

Mike Murdock writes that you have to inventory the seeds you already possess. He writes, "A seed is a tiny beginning with a huge future. It is anything that can become more. It is the beginning. It is anything that you can do, know or possess that can bless somebody else. Your thoughts are seeds for desired behavior, conduct and creativity. Your love is a seed. Your time is a seed. Your patience is a seed. Your money is a seed. Your kindness is a seed. Your prayers are seeds. Stopping slander is a seed. Forgiveness is a seed. Thankfulness is a seed. Your seed is anything you have received from God that can be traded for something else. You are a walking warehouse of seeds."

Murdock goes on to say, "Most people do not even know this. They have no idea how many seeds they contain. They can be planted in the lives of others. Anything that improves another is a seed. Anything that makes another smile is a seed. Anything that makes someone's life easier is a seed. Millions are so busy studying what they do not have, they overlook something they have already received."That is so true. Many of us are so busy focusing on the lack all around us that we need to stop and inventory the seeds that we have. Those seeds are able to multiply your life. They can bring you out of the hole you're in, or bring you out of the debt you're in. You have debt-canceling seeds within your possession. If you plant those seeds and begin to use everything you have as a resource that God can use, then truly you will be unlimited in your life. The miracle didn't happen in the master's hand; it happened in the hands of the disciples. It is time for you to multiply, be fruitful and increase.

9

A PRISONER OF GREAT EXPECTATION

---◆---

"We dream the dream in the midst of captivity."
"Your dream is the prophet that can profit your future."

Zechariah 9:12 says, "Come back to the place of safety, all you prisoners who still have hope! I promise this very day that I will repay two blessings for each of your troubles." I haven't heard many people use this Scripture, but it holds an incredible promise for us today. We need a strong anchor for our lives. I love the little saying that is upstream from Niagara Falls in a particular part of the river. Before people go over the falls they read a little sign that says, "Do you have an anchor?" There is another sign right after it that reads, "Do you know how to use it?" I am convinced like never before that we need an anchor and we need to know how to use it. Our lives need to be anchored to the right truths. We need to be anchored to great expectations, hope, and promise.

Today, we have economic upheaval, earthquakes, and political threats spreading throughout our world, and people are running in fear. But we can look to Zechariah 9:12 for hope and strength. It's an inconspicuous word in the Bible that can be a major anchoring point for us during these times.

Come back, the Scripture says, to the place of safety. The Scripture identifies the place of safety, as a place of our hope. He uses the word "prisoner" implying that we are imprisoned by hope. The greatest prison you can be in is the prison of hope. We can think of so many other prisons that people live in today—prisons of fear, prisons of pain, prisons of failure, prisons of past mistakes, or prisons of personal compromise. What prison are you in today? The kind of bondage that Zechariah is talking about is a good bondage. When everything is bound around you and everything else is falling apart, you can stay bound to the hope you have been given in Christ. He says this is your place of safety. Whatever you forfeit in life, do not let go of your hope; do not sacrifice your hope in God.

Remember the reflections of the psalmist who said in Psalm 43:5 NKJV "And why are you disquieted within me?" He spoke to his inner self, his emotions, and told himself to have hope in God. We have to stay anchored to the hope we have in Christ. Whatever has you captive has power over you. Whatever you are meditating on the most holds you captive. Your dominant thoughts control your atmosphere. Your dominant thoughts control your life, and who you are tomorrow is a direct result of your most dominant thoughts today.

People are intrigued by knowing the future. I can save you a lot of money, headaches, and trouble and tell what your future looks like. Whatever is inside of you right now is what your future will look like. A new thought, a new desire, a new design, or a new vision on the inside of you will reveal your potential future. Whatever you are carrying on the inside is what you will be tomorrow on the outside.

Whatever holds you captive has the right to rule your life. Zechariah invites us into the prison of hope. He invites us to be chained to hope, to be bound to hope, to be bound to expectation. Expectation is the only magnet that attracts the miracle provisions that God has promised to us. God has an incredible "super magnet" that He uses to bring blessings into our lives. It is called the force of expectation. Expectation is glorified faith, and its root, faith, is expecting good things to happen to you. It is a positive expectation. Fear, of course, is negative expectation. So faith becomes the magnet that attracts miracle provision from every source. Whatever miracle you need, your positive and persistent expectation will draw it into your life.

Jesus did not stop to reward talent or personality at any time in the four gospels. But when He saw faith, it impressed Him. Faith got His attention. He always stopped to acknowledge positive expectations. Before every major miracle that Jesus performed in the four gospels, faith was there. As Jesus was teaching one day, He said there was faith in the crowd. Jesus was walking through the street one day, and a woman pulled on His garment. Jesus asked who touched Him; He found faith in the crowd. God has a great sensitivity for positive expectations.

Rather than trying to change your life and fix all your problems and reverse everything that is wrong and figure how you are going to stay afloat, do everything you can to incorporate positive expectation into your life. If expectation is the magnet that draws the miracle provision, then you need to do everything you can to bring expectation into your life. The Word of God says, "So then faith cometh by hearing, and hearing by the word of God" (Romans 10:17 kjv). The more faith we need, the more Word we have to get because the Word is the source of positive expectation. Hebrews

11:3 says that the worlds were framed by faith. God built the world He wanted, and you can frame your world with positive expectations in the Word. Let the Word build expectations of a new future.

Your dream is the prophet of your future, and whatever you are carrying right now on the inside of you is declaring what your tomorrow will to be like. Don't sell out to a bad vision. Don't sell out to strongholds of fear. Don't compromise your positive expectations with negative meditations.

Return, Zechariah says, go back. The people had drifted from a place of hope. They had drifted from positive expectations. The prophet called them back. This book, *Fearonomics*, is calling you back. Come back to hope. Be grounded in the hope of Christ.

Paul wrote in Ephesians 3:1,2 NIV, "For this reason I, Paul, the prisoner of Christ Jesus for the sake of you Gentiles—Surely you have heard about the administration of God's grace that was given to me for you." Paul called himself a prisoner of Christ. He did not say he was a prisoner to man or he was a prisoner to the Roman government. He never acknowledged man's chains. He never acknowledged what man could do or let them put a lid on his life or his future. He constantly acknowledged that he was a prisoner to Someone else. My bond to Jesus is stronger. My connection to Jesus is stronger than my connection to man or to this life or to my possessions.

There's a play on words here. Become a prisoner of Jesus and a prisoner of hope. It's not possible to be chained to Jesus and be sad. You cannot be chained to Jesus and be discouraged. If you are Christ's prisoner, then you are in a jail of hope. You are in a prison of faith. Come out singing, "I've got a feeling that everything is going to be all right." Be committed to hope.

I have not been behind bars myself, but I have visited some prisoners. It is an incredibly eerie feeling when you walk into those dark, concrete slab walls and the big metal gate slams behind you. It feels as if you have been committed. It gives a whole new meaning to the word *commitment*.

When a bride and groom say their vows, you never hear them say, "I'll try. I'll try, till death do us part." It is always, "I do." I don't think many women or men would want to spend the rest of their lives with someone who is simply going to "try." Marriage is a commitment, and just as marriage is a commitment, we have to vow to be people of hope. We have to commit to the hope that Christ has birthed within us. At some point in your life, you will no longer be holding on to your dream, but your dream will be holding on to you. Keep hope alive.

We love to go out and fish. Sometimes the trip requires live bait. When you use live bait, you have to have a live well aerator that pumps oxygen where the shrimp or minnows are, and the aerator keeps the shrimp alive until you are ready to use them. A dream is a lot like the aerator that keeps the bait alive. We have to have an aerator for our dream too, something that pumps oxygen into the dream.

The Word of God is one way to keep a dream alive. Meditating on the dream is another method. Visit your dream place frequently, by going there spiritually and mentally, and think about the future you desire. When that dream finally becomes part of you, then it is no longer head knowledge but heart knowledge. You become what the book of James calls "a doer of the Word," a man who "shall be blessed in his deeds." (James 1:22-25.) This is the point where you are not holding on to a dream; the dream is sustaining you. It's an awesome thing to be able to say you are living the dream. If you meditate on your dream long enough and you keep it in your heart, you will come to an incredible place where the dream holds you. You have to make the transfer from head knowledge, to heart knowledge, into actually being a doer of the Word. When you do the Word, it produces incredible blessings in your life.

I had a couple in premarital counseling several years ago. Sometimes I go through different Scriptures, and show what the Bible says about marriage, and quote different authors and authorities. As we were going through the session, the groom-to-be would finish just about every statement I tried to make. Just about every time I started to quote Scripture, he would quote it better than I could. After about thirty minutes into the session, I said, "You don't need me. You are ready to get married. Obviously, you have all the answers."

I went away amused, thinking *I hope this is heart knowledge and not head knowledge.* Unfortunately a couple of years later, the couple divorced. This is proof that you can have all the knowledge on any particular subject, but you don't necessarily have the wisdom to know how to apply it. Applied knowledge is power. Don't just have a dream in your head; have a dream in your heart, one you can live out. You'll need to walk out your dream every day you live. Then you are on your way. When your dream makes the twelve-inch transfer from head to heart, incredible things begin to happen.

Psalm 126:1-5 says,

When the LORD brought back his exiles to Jerusalem,
    it was like a dream!
We were filled with laughter,
    and we sang for joy.

And the other nations said,

"What amazing things the LORD has done for them."

Yes, the LORD has done amazing things for us!

What joy!

Restore our fortunes, LORD,

as streams renew the desert.

Those who plant in tears

will harvest with shouts of joy.

Scripture says that when the Lord returned His children from their captivity, it was like a dream. When you are captive to your dream, then you can't be captivated by anything else. Your life is filled up. Your life is consumed with the plan and the will and the agenda that God has given you. When you have a positive, consuming hope about your life, your finances, your future, and your career, then the negativity all around you cannot touch you. There was bondage all around Jerusalem, but God's people declared, "We dream the dream in the midst of captivity." They were captive to a stronger bondage: hope. Their dream took them to restored fortunes. As streams renew the desert, God would renew them.

The passage goes on to say that many of us have planted in tears, but we will harvest with shouts of joy. Many of us in our pain have sown seeds and it seems as if nothing is happening; but the Lord promised that you would reap with shouts of joy. He promised that you would come again, singing, and return with a harvest. You will return with more than you had before. God is a God of restored fortunes.

The latter portion of Zechariah 9:12 says that God is going to give us double for our trouble. This promise is conditional; you have to stay a prisoner of hope. Throw away the key. This is not a come-

and-go situation. You are committed, and God has said you can't just come and go. You can't be up today and down tomorrow. You can't believe in the hope today and abandon the hope tomorrow. This dream has to be in you. You have to be consumed by it. You have to be willing to pursue it with every fiber of your being. Unless you are totally committed to that dream, it will not come to pass, and it will not come to pass to the extent that God desires. That dream has to be big on the inside of you and greater than anything on the outside of you.

10
I'M NOT WHAT I'VE BEEN THROUGH

———————◆———————

When I was a high school freshman, I played basketball with the varsity squad. Those guys were all tall and fast, and I felt honored to just be in the crowd. Once a week we had a free-throw competition, and whoever won would get a cool pair of team socks. At that time, I was a young man, just getting turned on to the Word. I remembered what Deuteronomy 28:8 said—*everything I touch is blessed.* When I would go to the free-throw line, I would say that Scripture under my breath—*everything that I touch is blessed. Since I am touching this basketball, then this basketball is blessed and because it is blessed, it has to go in that basket.* I would stand there thinking *Greater is He that is in me than he that is in the world.* It was kind of a David and Goliath situation when I looked at the height and ability of the other players who stood around that free-throw line. I remember winning several of those free-throw competitions in the midst of much older teammates. I believe it was because I visualized the ball going into the basket. I saw the greater One inside me, and the dream on the inside was greater than the opposition on the outside.

You have not yet lived your best day. The Church has not yet seen its best day. There is a hope that lies within you. There is a dream that God has placed in your heart. There is something that God needs done that He put you on the earth to do, and God called *you* to do it. There is something unfulfilled in your life. Keep your hope!

Look at Romans 5:1-2: "Therefore, since we have been made right in God's sight by faith, we have peace with God because of what Jesus Christ our Lord has done for us. Because of our faith, Christ has brought us into this place of undeserved privilege where we now stand, and we confidently and joyfully look forward to sharing God's glory." We are people of confidence. We look joyfully toward God's glory. We have an inward expectation that things could change at any moment. Romans 5:5 says, "And this hope will not lead to disappointment. For we know how dearly God loves us, because he has given us the Holy Spirit to fill our hearts with his love." Our hope leads to fulfillment and an experience with the Holy Spirit. Zechariah's declaration to stay imprisoned by hope is the method that keeps our lives insulated from disappointment, letdown, and upset. As long as we are with God, we have a sense of hope. Through trials, character tests, and tough life events, we keep hope alive.

Hope keeps us anchored on the horizon. To avoid seasickness, you have to keep your eyes focused on the horizon. To avoid life sickness, you have to keep your eyes focused on hope.

The word "hope" here provides an intriguing word study. The word "hope" comes from the Greek *dokimas*, which means "character." It implies that something has been put to the test and has measured up. In Israel if you pick up a piece of pottery and look at the bottom, it reads *dokiamos*, meaning "approved." It passed the furnace test. This isn't obvious to the casual reader, but the person who understands Greek can see that this type of hope has passed the test. How can you stay in your seat right now? You have to be up in your living room, running around, shouting that God has given us a hope, and that hope has passed the furnace test. It has measured up and proven to produce time and time again.

Zechariah declared, "I will give you double for your trouble, but return to your anchor, O prisoner of hope. Return to your refuge, O prisoner of hope, because your hope has measured up." (Zechariah 9:12.) Hope passed the furnace test. It has been approved by God, approved for use in every situation of life. Our bad circumstances just cause hope to shine; they cause positive expectations of faith to rise because we have a proven faith. We have a proven hope.

We are not just building our lives on some fantasy, like many people who are negative toward Christianity. They say Christianity is just a crutch, but Christianity is only as strong as what holds it up. Christianity won't buckle under pressure. They may call it a crutch, but it has been proven on the shoulders of Old Testament prophets, on Christ Himself, and by infallible evidence and miracles. We have been given a proven faith upon which we can stand. Psalm 69:33 KJV says, "The LORD...despiseth not his prisoners." When you are a prisoner to a vision and refuse to compromise your stance, the Lord will not despise you. He will not turn His back on His prisoners. He is faithful to uphold His people.

We are talking about a dream, a hope, and a vision. There are three qualities that a dream from God has.

1. When it is a God dream, you can't shake it. It's not because of the pizza or the Mexican food you ate last night. You can't shake a

God dream. It's with you when you wake up. It's with you when you go to bed and all hours in between. The dream is in you, it's on you, and it defines you. It's who you are. You can't quit the dream and the dream doesn't quit you. We have all had days when we just wanted to give up. Sometimes it looks as if more is against us than for us. Just because you want to smash the plates, sell the kids, drown the husband, yank down the drapes, put a brick through the TV, keep driving past work, go to the woods, or trade your wife for a hound dog, doesn't change the fact that you have a dream in your life from God. The Scripture says that if you will stay anchored to that, you will discover a place of restored fortunes.

Joel 2:28 says, "Then, after doing all those things, I will pour out my Spirit upon all people. Your sons and daughters will prophesy. Your old men will dream dreams, and your young men will see visions." When the Holy Spirit works in your life, you will have dreams and visions, not just goose bumps. The Holy Spirit deposits a vision in your heart that He made you a steward of, and nobody else can fulfill that on the earth. As we said earlier, there is something that God needs to have done, and He put you on the earth to do it. Dreams and visions are a result of the Holy Spirit being able to work in our lives. The Holy Spirit can only work if we are yielded vessels made available to Him.

Revelation 1:10 has a powerful phrase that some skim over. It says John was in the Spirit on the Lord's Day. Getting in the presence of God at the right time enables us to see what God is showing us and hear what God is saying. Many times we don't stop to get into His atmosphere on the Lord's Day. There is a Lord's Day for each and every one of us, and we pray that those days become more frequent. But the big question is: are we in position to receive the Holy Spirit?

When you are in the same location as a pastor for several years, you tend to cycle through different revelations. You will say similar things over time, but you always struggle for originality. People come to me from time to time and say, "That was a great word," and "That really helped me; it really blessed my life." Sometimes I chuckle on the inside because these same people heard me say that before— maybe two years previously or two months ago. It was the same word, but they weren't the same person in the same place. Sometimes the word can be as true as true can be, but we are not yet in a position to receive it. One of our jobs is staying in a position where we can hear the right word at the right time. If we do that, the word will nurture our dreams, aerating the vision and the hope that anchors us.

When the Spirit is on you, just like when John was in the Spirit in the Lord's Day, you see more, not less. God is always the God of more. In the 1930s they started a motion in Congress to close the U.S. Patent Office on the premise that there were no new things under the sun. They thought that everything that could possibly be invented had been invented and the patent office was an expense that the government didn't need. So they passed a motion to close it. I think about that today—how many people have quit on a dream and given up on a vision?

You cannot shake a vision that God has given. You've got to dream beyond today. You may be going through something and you want to close the patent office on creativity, but you have to keep nurturing your dream and fanning the flame of the vision that God has given you. The bottom line is that your God-given dream is your anchor. That is your stability. If you let that go, you are inviting havoc into your life. You will create all sorts of trouble for yourself when you are not doing the things that bring God pleasure.

2. You become the vision you meditate on. You take on the characteristics of your vision. It defines you. When you say movies, you think Steven Spielberg. When you say basketball, you think Michael Jordan. Similarly, when you think about your dream, you become the first thing that comes into your mind. You become your vision. The vision takes on a life of its own. Whatever you keep before you constantly, you will eventually become. What you think about, you bring about.

3. It defines you. It has been said that if you can hold on to a dream for five years it will happen, but you have to be willing to hold on to it for that time frame. God is looking for people who can do the impossible. What a pity that we plan only what we can do by ourselves.

When Abraham Lincoln was assassinated, investigators listed the things they found on his body. The night he was assassinated he was carrying a small handkerchief, a penknife, five dollars, a spectacle case, and a newspaper clipping. The newspaper clipping called Lincoln the greatest statesman of all time. Abraham Lincoln faced great opposition on his way to the presidency. He faced a great deal of adversity, and had many critics. Lincoln found this short piece written in a newspaper that called him the greatest statesman of all time. No doubt he would have taken that out and rehearsed it and meditated on it to keep his dream alive and to keep his self-esteem built up.

That is what we do with the Word of God. When we read the Word of God, we are reading God's love letter. It is His Word to us and spells out what He thinks about us. It is His heart concerning us. These are the things that He wants to see happen in our lives if He could just get us to believe them. If He can just get us, like Abraham

Lincoln, to carry the truth in our hearts and minds, then we will become our vision and it will define us. When people say your name, they will associate you with the dream that you're carrying in your heart.

GOD LOVES YOU

Let's talk about entering the field of dreams. Genesis 37 tells the story of Joseph. Joseph's father gave him a coat. This coat represents a coat of favor. It was a revelation of how much his father loved him. In Genesis 37:5, Joseph dreamed a dream. He is a model dreamer in Scripture. That is why we talk about him so much. For Joseph, the beautiful coat of many colors was a constant reminder of the favor and love of his father.

When we look to Scripture, we can see that God has given us many things to help us understand how much He loves us. God gives us dreams and vision. He gave us the cloak of righteousness. He covered us with salvation. He gives us continuous reminders of His love and commitment to us, and those reminders release the life force and potential on the inside of us. It is as if God steps back and beholds His creation and celebrates who we are. He celebrates the gift that He made us to be to the world around us.

Recently, I was doing some work on the house. Some of the outside doors had weathered with time, so I decided I would sand them down and put a new coat of lacquer on them and shine them up a little bit. It was a lengthy process; it was not something I could do in five minutes—which is a challenge for me because I like things to come together quickly, just like every other red-blooded American male. I blocked out the time I needed and started sanding the doors down and making sure all the rough edges were smoothed out. Then I applied the lacquer coat and then the second coat. After it was done, I stepped back and looked at the doors. I was so proud at how bright and shiny they were, restored so they looked like new. I was kind of beholding my creation, if you will. I thought about how God must view us and how He must step back and look at us and say, "That is My creation. Those are the ones I made and formed by My Spirit and breathed My life into." Dreamers need a continual reminder of the favor of God in order to keep their dream alive.

ALL THINGS ARE POSSIBLE

You have to believe that all things are possible. God gave Joseph a dream of greatness. In order for you to see God's dream fulfilled in your life, you have to believe that all things are possible. Your dream here on earth has to connect with a heavenly vision. This is a divine chemistry. He authorized the dream already and set it in motion before the foundation of the world. When your earthly dream lines up with His heavenly vision, watch out—it is a cataclysmic experience. He will rush resources into your life. The divine magnet of favor will cause things to come to you, and powerful things will happen. So we need to seek His heavenly vision for our lives and let His vision modify what we plan to do.

GET READY FOR RESISTANCE

Resistance is a part of every dream. It's the price of admission to our field of dreams. The field of dreams is not cheap, and not everyone will be willing to walk through the resistance to get to the field of dreams. The Scripture teaches us that Joseph's brothers despised him. He had to go down and check on his brothers at Shechem. Shechem indicates a place of bad memories; it was there that his sister, Dina, was raped. It was a place of bitterness and hurt.

For you to enter your field of dreams, you have to go back through a place of pain. You have to slay your pain, your memory of loss, your feelings of regret, and your fear of failure. Some of you may have launched businesses that didn't work out. You had dreams that were never fulfilled. You may have tried to get on the inventors' circuit. That didn't work out; the invention blew up, and smoke went everywhere. You have to visit your place of pain and bury your painful memories once and for all before you can enter your field of dreams. Your pain cannot go with you there. Your dream has to live in a place free from past pain and failure. That is where dreams thrive.

In the midst of this situation, Joseph's brothers were very jealous, and they tried to manipulate him. They tried to frame him. They tried everything they could do to stop him. They threw him in a pit and sold him into slavery. What is interesting in the process is that Joseph's brother Judah was the one who stood up and said, "Don't kill him; spare his life." The other brothers would have killed Joseph, but Judah spoke up. This illustrates a powerful truth: Judah means "praise." Praise keeps your dream alive. How do you keep your dream alive when everything looks messed up? When everyone around you says you are crazy? How do you keep your dream alive when you are the only one keeping it on life support, and you don't have people around you to help you fulfill it? You keep it alive with praise, saying, "Thank You, Lord; You're the Author of the dream. You're the Giver of life. God, invigorate this dream, aerate this dream, keep it alive. As I worship You, I thank You, God, that it will come to pass with Your power." Worship your dream into being. Praise in the midst of difficult situations; praise to keep the dream alive. Worship and sing the song of the Lord because you will remember not only what God has done, but also what God is doing and what God will continue to do. You cannot stop a dreamer.

I love this Scripture about Joseph found in Genesis 39:21-23:

> But the LORD was with Joseph in the prison and showed him his faithful love. And the LORD made Joseph a favorite with the prison warden. Before long, the warden put Joseph in charge of all the other prisoners and over everything that happened in the prison. The warden had no more worries, because Joseph took care of everything. The LORD was with him and caused everything he did to succeed.

The phrase, "the Lord was with Joseph," is something you find over and over in the story of Joseph's life. How do you build a life in which the Lord is constantly with you? It's when your earthly dream lines up with His heavenly vision. The Lord is with you through the process. You can go through many adverse situations but the Lord is still with you. The Lord remained with Joseph, and He reminded him of His faithful love. Because the Lord was with him, it caused everything he did to succeed. It seems to me that if God did not want us to succeed, He would have let Joseph have a disastrous life. This could have been a terrible story, but Joseph kept the reality of God's love alive. He didn't have to get out of the pit; he could have died there. He didn't have to get past slavery; they could have beaten him to death. He didn't have to get out of prison; he could have stayed there for life. He could have been unable to get away from Potiphar's wife; he could have compromised. There are so many other endings to this story we could write besides success, but when you've got God working with you, you will have success. Joseph came to the point where he wasn't holding on to the dream; the dream was holding on to him. When we can get to that point, we will be able to rejoice in any situation.

Dreamers need to overcome several obstacles:

1. Dreamers have to deal with immaturity, small thinkers, and people who don't see life on the same scale. Other people don't see the same vision that you see. Never try to convince small thinkers of your big vision. That is what I love about Jesus' ministry. Joyce Meyer pointed this out to me the other day. Jesus did not waste His time trying to convince His critics that He was right. He preached the gospel and kept His heart in the right place. He stayed centered, and He kept moving forward. So don't respond to the immature by becoming immature yourself. Small thinkers will never understand your heart or vision.

2. Dreamers have to deal with personal attacks and criticism. Rock throwers will want to stand outside and throw rocks at your glass house. The key to that is: don't live in a glass house. Have a resilient personality. Have divine buoyancy, as I say, because Satan may try to push you under the water and drown you. But believers are like a fishing bobber; we always pop back up to the surface. We always emerge stronger than we were before. Don't allow personal attacks or criticism to discourage you. Don't modify your behavior just because everybody thinks you're crazy. We have all been attacked personally. I can remember in the formative years of my ministry receiving many more attacks than encouragement. Some people want to put you in a box and tell you how to do things. They want to tell you that you are wrong. They don't find the good in it; they can only see the bad. Keep your spirit strong, and stay sweet in your attitude. Use prayer to keep your mind free from the damage of personal attacks and people's criticism.

3. Dreamers have to deal with envy. People are going to be envious, just like Joseph's brothers were. They didn't have the same dream that he did. The key to staying free from envy is to know that everyone's dream is different. Everyone's vision is different. God deals with people on different terms and in different ways. He has a unique dream for you, and He wants you to seek Him until that dream is revealed in your heart. When you celebrate other people's dreams, God will give you your own dream to celebrate.

4. Avoid negative pitfalls. Avoid the temptation to go off road, so to speak, and go negative and land in the ditch. History records that Joseph was the only man in history to become the warden while an inmate. God sent someone with a need in the midst of Joseph's need. God uses somebody else's need to give us an opportunity to get out of our bondage. Success is finding a need and meeting it. We need to ask God to deal with us the way He dealt with Joseph. Look at Genesis 40:5-8:

> While they were in prison, Pharaoh's cup-bearer and baker each had a dream one night, and each dream had its own meaning. When Joseph saw them the next morning, he noticed that they both looked upset. "Why do you look so worried today?" he asked them.
>
> And they replied, "We both had dreams last night, but no one can tell us what they mean."
>
> "Interpreting dreams is God's business," Joseph replied. "Go ahead and tell me your dreams."

Notice how God showed His power in the strangest of places. Joseph was in prison, but he was incarcerated not by bars of steel or man's commandment. He was incarcerated to the dream of God.

He was bound to the dream. An opportunity finds him while he is prison. I am telling you, in your bondage there is an opportunity. I love what Joseph said—he said interpreting dreams is God's business. He's given us the ability to understand the dream of our lives. In verse 8 the *King James* says, "Do not interpretations belong to God?" Be a dreamer's friend and ask the Lord what He wants for this situation. *How do You want me to sow in this situation? How do You want me to invest in this situation?* How you handle your natural circumstances will determine how strongly you are anchored to the hope of God. If you can stay faithful, then God will deliver you from your negative situation.

Time and time again, we've seen the supernatural hand of God in our ministry, especially in the building phases. The supernatural hand of God was on us even when we did not have the funds for the project. We just went ahead and planned anyway. We set the wheels in motion. We said we were going to buy the materials. We didn't have all the money we needed, but we were going to buy that material by faith. Our most recent project was a $900,000 sanctuary expansion, and God was with us every step of the way. We said "OK, we are going to pour the foundation," and we thought it would stay empty a long time. Then supernaturally, unexpectedly, there was the money to put up the building shell. $50,000 came in, and then another $20,000. I said, "Well, that shell can sit there a long time." Then the money for lumber came in. We had to knock down a big wall. We had a big banner on the wall that said, "Beyond the Walls." The day we knocked that wall down was a great day, as we saw the big old wall fall and the dust fly everywhere. We did not push the wall down; the dream caused the wall to fall. What had just been a plan on paper for ten years became a reality because we took steps toward it. Know that God will interpret your dreams for you. He will show you how your dream relates to your life and He'll build a bridge of deliverance out of your situation.

An interesting thing happened on 9/11 starting on the seventy-eighth floor of the south tower. Sylvian Ramsondar, 31, had a collapsed lung, a broken collarbone, and a piece of metal the size of a playing card lodged near his aorta. On the fiftieth floor he said he wanted to rest, but a stranger said, "If you can make it, let's keep going." He kept saying that everything was going to be all right. Mr. Ramsondar found himself in a terrible situation. Everything inside him said give up. He didn't know that that building would collapse very soon, but a stranger came by and said keep going, keep going, everything is going to be all right. It kept him going, from the fiftieth floor all the way to the first floor. He was motivated to keep going despite his bleeding, a broken collar bone and a collapsed lung because a voice of encouragement kept him going, led him to safety, and saved his life. We never know what is coming down the road, but God will put people in our lives to encourage us to keep going.

Three years after his 1996 cancer diagnosis, Lance Armstrong won the Tour de France, finishing seven minutes ahead of his nearest competitor. His victory sent his sent a message that cancer is not a death sentence; he was stronger physically than he was before. When we stay true to our dreams, like Joseph—who became the right-hand man to Pharaoh—then God has a plan for our futures. In your current situation, it may not look like it. When we look at our country right now and we see all that is going on, the negatives can build a wall around us. We need to realize that God has a plan.

It is time for men and women to take a stand. Stand against the giants of debt, the negative reports about your future and your children's future, the doom and gloom about retirement, and lost savings. Rise up like Lance Armstrong and send a message to others who are suffering in silence. We are not going to sit here until we die. We are not going to perish with the bad reports. We are going to rise, invest in the land, and hear from the Lord.

Interpretations belong to the Lord. The *New Living Translation* says that interpreting dreams is God's business. These are perfect times for the Lord. God thrives in times like this, and His people should thrive as well because He gives us the power to interpret His dreams for us. When you don't know what to do, you can know that God has the answer. The missing link between failure and success is the presence of God. Be like John and get into the presence of the Lord on the Lord's Day.

The prophet Joel showed how the Spirit of the Lord can bring you dreams and visions. The apostle Paul was chained to two Roman guards, one on his right and one on his left, yet he would lift his voice and say, "I'm a prisoner to Christ. I'm a prisoner to something more significant. I'm a prisoner to something greater; I'm a prisoner to hope, to positive expectation. If I stay anchored to that hope, to that trust, nothing that man can do can move me." Nothing that this life throws at you can move you. Let me be like that stranger who came alongside the man injured in the world trade center on 9/11. You may feel as if you are on the fiftieth floor and bleeding, and there is no way you can make it. Let me come alongside you today and say, "You can make it. You can finish. Everything is going to be all right. God is with you." And if God is with you, who can be against you?

11
PASSING THE IMMUNITY CHALLENGE

———◆———

*"No, I beat my body and make it my slave so that after I have preached
to others, I myself will not be disqualified for the prize."*

1 Corinthians 9:27 NIV

On the TV reality show *Survivor*, the tribe that wins doesn't
have to go to the tribal council where they vote someone off
the show. Similarly, if we don't pass the immunity challenge, we
could be eliminated from the race. The word *immune* means "to be
free, exempt from, marked by protection, having a high degree of
resistance to disease." In this life, God wants us to be free. He wants
us to be exempt from attacks of the enemy. God wants us to be
marked by protection.

We have to learn how to go through the tests and trials of life,
and live our lives so that we can survive daily immunity challenges.
The apostle Paul said you might be disqualified, to be declared unfit,
incapable of continuing. As he said in verse 27, "No, I beat my
body." We discipline our lives so that we can win the challenge and
come into the freedom that God has for us.

Paul's body and emotions were not controlling him. He might have an impulse to eat a piece of chocolate cake, but he didn't eat the whole cake. His impulses might tempt him in a former addiction, but they didn't control him. He said, I make my appetites and my desires my slave. I bring these things into slavery and control, so that after I have preached to others I myself will not be disqualified from the prize.

Followers of Christ should want to be a bright light in the world. That is the ultimate prize, the reason we're here. We want to be the last man standing, to have our torches lit at the end of the game. Paul said his biggest worry was that after he told others how to live for God that in the end he wouldn't be able to live up to what he preached.

We go through many "immunity challenges" in our lives. But in God, once you stand your ground and pass the test, you become immune to that challenge. When God gives you victory, you don't ever have to go back and deal with that same thing again. God wants you to be able to use that challenge to help other people. God brought you through a bad marriage, a terrible addiction, or a problem with your child. Now you can tell others how God brought you through it. You can tell them how you were able to praise God on a good day, but then also how you got out of bed on a bad day and lifted your hands to God and said, God I praise You anyway! Don't let the enemy disqualify your witness after you have stood for the Lord. Don't end up standing outside of the righteousness of God. The Bible declares, "To the pure, all things are pure ..." (Titus 1:15 NIV).

Two thoroughbred racehorse owners were always trying to get the better of each other. Every year they would host a steeplechase race. So one of the owners decided that year he would go out and hire a professional jockey to ride his horse. He thought if he hired a professional jockey, he'd be sure to win the race.

When the shoot opened, the horses came out, but about halfway through, both horses fell on the ground. It was a terrible wipeout. Since the riders were skilled and the horses were strong, the riders got back up on the horses and galloped to the finish. The owner burst into the stable area and the professional jockey said, "We won! We did it! We did it, I told you I could win it for you!"

The owner replied, "You fool! You won, but you were on the wrong horse!"

In the confusion of the fall, he had mounted the wrong horse! He may have won, but he finished on the wrong horse! We don't want to be disqualified in the end because we were riding the wrong horse. We may have crossed the line and finished, but we didn't do it God's way, we didn't adhere to God's truth or follow God's promises.

THE FIRST IMMUNITY DESTROYER: DISTRACTION

There are three personality traits that can destroy immunity. For the first trait, look at Hebrews 11:24, 25 KJV, talking about Moses: "By faith Moses, when he was come to years, refused to be called the son of Pharaoh's daughter; Choosing rather to suffer affliction with the people of God, than to enjoy the pleasures of sin for a season."

How many of you have made that your determination? That you'd rather suffer affliction? Jesus taught that we would be persecuted for His name's sake, in Matthew 5 in the Sermon on the Mount. The term *persecuted* or *afflicted*, means to be persecuted for being close to God or being a witness for God, it's persecuted for your faith.

Moses chose to be afflicted or misunderstood for his stance with God, rather than choose the pleasures of sin for a season. Let me tell you, sin is pleasurable. Sin is fun. "How do you know sin is fun, Pastor Mark?" Because so many people are doing it. Sin is pleasurable. The Bible says it. I didn't read anything into it, and I didn't write it. Sin is pleasurable, but it's only pleasurable for a season. After the pleasure and the luster of it wears off, you have to carry the condemnation, judgment, bitterness, and baggage around for a long, long time.

Hebrews 11:26 KJV says: "Esteeming the reproach of Christ greater riches than the treasures in Egypt: for he had respect unto the recompense of the reward." The word respect there is very powerful. In the original, it's the word "look." This is what Moses did to sustain himself in an evil word. He esteemed or laid honor on God instead of on the world around him. I'd rather be persecuted with Christ than praised by the world. I'd rather be persecuted with Christ, than loved, accepted and affirmed, knowing that I was going to hell as I was being affirmed. I would rather be in the company of the righteous knowing that I'm going to go through some stuff, than be disqualified. If I can make it through this season of persecution, God has something better for me.

So Moses honored and esteemed the reproach of Jesus Christ. Hebrews 11:26 KJV says: "…for he had respect unto the recompense of the reward." He looked for the reward in it. Moses looked past his current struggles and looked for the reward. God has a reward for those who do the right thing. God has a reward for those who live right and make the right choices. He has a reward for those who follow His moral code and His moral system. He has a reward! The Bible said Moses looked for the reward in it. That's why we have so many down-in-the-mouth, baptized-in-lemon-juice believers. They can't find the joy and the reward. Sometimes our culture, our childhood, or our church environment makes us think that God is mad. God is gloomy and upset with you. He can't wait until you get to His house so we can all be sad and gloomy and condemned together. Bless God, when you get to His house, He's going to straighten you up!

But Moses looked for the reward. He looked for the joy and knew that the reproach of Christ was greater than to be praised and loved as the fair-haired child of the Egyptians. He chose God's plan for his life. God is calling you and me today to look for something different. Look in a different direction. The word *look*, or *he looked* in the original Greek, means "to look away from everything else in order to look intently upon a brand new subject or object." This is what happens when you fast and pray. Moses looking, according to the Greek text, was not so much looking *to*, but it was *looking away* so that he could look to. This is the first personal trait that can flunk you out of immunity: distraction. Moses didn't allow himself to get distracted. He looked away from the pleasures of sin so he could more adequately focus on God and God's purpose for his life.

We get stronger when we look away. We've gone through a few 21-day fasts here at Livingway Family Church. Because I practiced the art of looking away from things like cookies and cakes and pies, fruit became my new dessert. Fruit is the new chocolate chip cookie. Yeah! Now, I would have never thought that I would make that statement. Ever! I have some German blood, and we Germans love our sweets. Some Germans love their beer, but I'm not that kind of German! When you look away from something, like dessert or soda or some other junk food, you develop your power to strengthen *healthy* desires. This needs to become a habit.

I used to love all sorts of bad food, but now it's nothing to me, it's like looking at dirt. There's no appeal to it. Why? Because for a season, I looked away. By passing the immunity challenge, those things have no draw or attraction for me any longer. That's how all sins and unhealthy appetites work. James 1:14 in the *Amplified* says, "But every person is tempted when he is drawn away, enticed and baited by his own evil desire (lust, passions)." Every person who's tempted is in an immunity challenge when they are drawn away and baited. That's the deceit of the enemy. He baits you a little bit at a time, until you're living in a whole new reality. It's seductive and subtle. The account of Genesis tells us about Satan's nature. He is the most subtle beast of the field. He is tricky and he baits you until it becomes an evil desire, a lust or a passion that draws you out into a realm where Satan can disqualify you.

The apostle Paul starts out by saying in 1 Corinthians 9:27 NIV, "I beat my body." Within the scripture's context, he's talking about an athlete, like a boxer or a marathon runner. It's a sports term: I beat my body, I discipline myself, I push it to the limit and then I push beyond. Paul was saying he practices in his spiritual life a discipline over his flesh, not indulging in whatever his flesh sees or letting it meditate on whatever it wants. Like Paul, we can discipline our minds, eyes, ears, and our time. When we do that, our time with God will be so great and so incredible that we will be protected from the things that Satan tries to do to us.

A lack of discipline might be fun at the moment, but it's only after a time of discipline that you can enter a season of fruitfulness. Hebrews 12:11 says: "No discipline is enjoyable while it is happening—it's painful! But afterward there will be a peaceful harvest of right living for those who are trained in this way." That's immunity. The test is designed to bring forth greater fruit. For example, the trees on the outer perimeter of the forest take a beating from the wind. They end up healthier, stronger, and more resilient because they've been through a testing period. If you have been through some testing and temptation, allow the Lord to be a Father to you. He can correct you and mentor you so that great things start to happen. When the Holy Spirit is your life coach, you'll pass the immunity challenge and come to a place where your life is yielding the fruit of a relationship with God. Your fruit will be flourishing and multiplying because you went through a period of testing.

Trouble comes when you're drawn away from God. You are tempted by your own lust, passion, and desires. You start to think you're really onto something but you find out it's really nothing at all. Had you waited on God, your life would have produced an abundant harvest and you would have had blessings on every hand.

THE SECOND IMMUNITY DESTROYER: LACK OF MOTIVATION

The second personality trait that destroys immunity is lack of motivation. 1 Corinthians 10:1 KJV says: "Moreover, brethren, I would not that ye should be ignorant, how that all our fathers were under the cloud, and all passed through the sea." All of the fathers had the same opportunity for blessing. All of them had passed under God's cloud of favor, but not all of them were recipients of it. The second trait that can flunk you out of your immunity challenge is to be "disinclined." Disinclined individuals lack the will or the motivation to continue. The Bible said they were all under the cloud, but watch what happened to them in 1 Corinthians 10:5-6 KJV emphasis mine: "But with many of them God was not well pleased: for they were overthrown [They were disqualified, they flunked the immunity challenge] in the wilderness. Now these things were our examples, to the intent we should not lust after evil things, as they also lusted." From verses 7 through 11, God gives the children of

Israel five reasons why they flunked their immunity challenge. They were all under the same cloud of God's favor, but that didn't mean they were all immune to a wilderness experience. It's just like people who go to the same church, week after week, experience the same worship week after week, and experience the same Word week after week, but so many of them are overthrown in a wilderness experience. Just because they're under God's cloud doesn't mean they're making the right decisions.

The wilderness you're walking through is different than the wilderness I'm walking through. God wants each of us to pass through our individual immunity tests and be able to cross the line and be qualified for the prize. He wants us to be able to say, "I went through the fire. I faced a difficult test in my life, but I stayed focused on God's plan for me." Don't allow your personal life, your family life, or your business life to get overthrown. Don't allow yourself to be disqualified by people who have lost their motivation and determination.

I love a quote from Booker T. Washington that said, "You can't hold a man down without staying down with the man." Be a people lifter. It was Mark Twain who said, "Stay away from people who belittle your ambition." Great people are the ones who tell you that you, too, can be great, and your life can bear the fruits of greatness. Don't hang around people who are de-motivated or disinclined. The disinclined and de-motivated in the body of Christ are happily content in their average. Somebody said recently that they've experienced a "Christian hardening of the arteries." Everything is passé; they have no flow of God in their lives, and no excitement. Their Christianity is diluted by a stupor of self. In other words, they're drunk with themselves!

God is not pleased with a disinclined attitude. All that the Israelites wanted to do was complain that Moses had brought them out in the desert. It wasn't enough that they were delivered from the mud pits, they wanted to find fault with God's deliverance. They found fault with the whole exodus plan. God said, *Why are you focusing on all of the negative? Why are you focusing on all of the trouble? Why are you so disinclined?*

"Well I'm not going out there, you go out there."

"Oh we're gonna lose anyway, let's just stay here and do nothing."

"Let's just stay here with all the other do-nothing's, all the other disinclined individuals, disenfranchised individuals."

You know the type: they can't go out and make a mark or do anything significant, so they just hang around and complain about everyone who does.

Success comes with a price. Prosperity comes with a price. The only time work follows success is in the dictionary. You're a bigger target now that you are prospering than you were when nobody knew your name. Now everybody's talking about you and running you down about what you're driving, what you're wearing, how you're living, and how you're running your business. They think you must be on drugs, or selling drugs, because you're too prosperous and there must be something wrong. They're jealous, disenfranchised, unmotivated, and belittle your ambition.

But how do you spot great people? They're the ones who say you, too, can be great and rise from the ashes! You, too, can get out of the projects and the slums, get off welfare, and have a great life! You, too, can have a great job, a great future, a great marriage, a great career, and have a great education. When you hang around with the motivated, they will motivate you to do more. We have great people to show us an example of how things can be for us.

First Corinthians 10:6 KJV says, "Now these things were our examples, to the intent we should not lust after evil things, as they also lusted." When we say that word *lust,* everybody starts freaking out and putting their own definitions on it. Let's just harness it in this way: their desires, appetites, and passions weren't in line with God's desires, appetites and passions. They desired something that God didn't desire for them. God puts passion in your heart to do something He wants to accomplish on the Earth. The Bible said, mark them as an example so that you won't be overthrown or disqualified in the same way. You will lose your influence and nobody will care about what you say if your lifestyle doesn't line up with your words. It's just like the old saying: your actions speak louder than your words. Don't be like the reality show contestants and have them say, "Sorry. Nice job, enjoy your parting gifts. You have been eliminated." It's always so cold how they say it on television, "Get your stuff, get on the plane and go home." Not in the morning, right now!

So many people have experienced those cold words in their life, that cold, stark reality. You do not pass go, you do not collect $200, that's it, game over. You're out. You've been disqualified. The word for *write* is a tremendous picture in the Greek. It's a word that comes from the old schoolhouse terminology. It means to write something down on the chalkboard, so that anyone can read it and copy it exactly. God said "write this down on the chalkboard of your heart, so that you can go out and copy it exactly. This is exactly what I want you to apply to your life." Can you say amen?

THE THIRD IMMUNITY DESTROYER: LACK OF ENDURANCE

The third immunity destroyer is lack of endurance. If people don't stick around long enough, they're disqualified, they don't pass go, they don't collect $200. I love the television commercial that has the guy with the homemade wings. He takes off from a bridge, and he's flying down through the river. Everyone watching him says, "ahhhh!" There's an old guy, kind of a disgruntled sort, who just kind of turns and starts walking away, and says, "Yeah, but he can't swim." He can fly, but he can't swim. So many times, we haven't made provision to be living for Jesus 20 years from now, 10 years from now, 5 years from now or even 2 years from now. We can fly, but can we swim? Can we sustain the presence of God? Can we sustain a move of God? In Exodus 33:15, Moses declared, *God, we will not move without your presence.* His presence is vital to our success. If you doubt this, just try life without God. You won't like it!

Are our daily lives so radiant with His glory that when we get together in worship, all you can see is the brightness of God's glory? Can our personal lives be so radiant with Him? When we come together, it's like a bonfire, a California forest fire out of control. No matter how many fire departments and helicopters that they use, no matter how much foam they drop from the sky, nothing can extinguish the radiance of God's power, because of the individual commitment that each one of us has to Christ.

God used Elisha to cleanse Naaman from leprosy. Naaman, after having received this incredible miracle healing, wanted to give Elisha something. 2 Kings 5:16 KJV says, "But he said, As the LORD liveth, before whom I stand, I will receive none. And he urged him to take it; but he [the prophet of God] refused." Elisha would not receive payment for the healing. It would have been payment for doing the will of God. But Elisha's servant, Gehazi had something in his heart that was not in the heart of his master. 2 Kings 5:20 goes on to say, "But Gehazi, the servant of Elisha the man of God, said, Behold, my master hath spared Naaman this Syrian, in not receiving at his hands that which he brought: but, as the LORD liveth, I will run after him, and take somewhat of him." Gehazi couldn't pass the immunity test. He should have had what was in the heart of his master. He should've carried that same love for God, but Gehazi's heart was not right and he couldn't pass the test. This is living the disciplined life, passing the immunity test of greed, lust, and convenience. We have to pass the immunity challenge of spiritual coldness and hardheartedness.

I love that word in Hebrews 12:4 where it says that none of us have resisted sin to the point of shedding blood. In Gethsemane, Jesus literally sweat drops of blood, in His struggle to resist sin. Luke 22:44 NIV says, "And being in anguish, he prayed more earnestly, and his sweat was like drops of blood falling to the ground." Sweating blood through the pores is a rare medical condition in which the capillaries open under extreme stress. It's highly unlikely that any of us have resisted sin to the degree that Jesus did in Gethsemane. Hebrews 12:3 says to consider Him who endured the cross.

None of you has resisted drugs or old addictions to the point that your capillaries have literally burst with blood. None of you has said no to your girlfriend who thinks it's okay to have sex before marriage, to the point that your pores begin to sweat great drops of blood. None of you has resisted the office secretary to such a degree that it required your shedding of blood. When they offered you bribe money and said, "if you'll just do this, I'll make you great, I'll remember you when I come into my kingdom," you kept your character because it violated your morals. You knew it violated your code of conduct and you said, no, I can't take this money. None of you have had to resist to the point that you literally sweat great drops of blood. At some point you have to conquer your pride, and say like Jesus did: *Lord God, I see what I'm up against. I would love for You to take it from me, but if You can't take it from me, give me strength to endure it so that I can go through it with dignity. I want to pass the test.*

The Son of God suffered for us, and He passed His immunity challenge. He has abundant life and the authority to reign and rule, because he passed the test. Gehazi didn't pass the test. Gehazi, the Bible said, got the same leprosy that was on Naaman. He wanted something that God didn't want him to have. His desires weren't right, he disobeyed, and he stepped out from God's protection. He got two bags of silver and two changes of clothing, but was it worth him having leprosy, his family having leprosy and his seed cursed forever? Absolutely not. If you are striving outside of God's will, you can get what you want, but you may not want what you get.

12
MORE THAN A SURVIVOR

———◆———

So we come, all of us, to the ultimate immunity challenge. When you choose the Son of God and His will, you have passed the greatest immunity challenge! Hell was yours, but now Heaven is yours, destruction was yours, but now restoration is yours. You have passed the test, you have found the Son, you have attained eternal life, and you are eternally exempt from shame and judgment. Because Jesus was judged for our sins, we never have to be judged for our sins again. We never have to be condemned for our sins again. Jesus was judged once for all so that we could have immunity.

Everybody's immunity challenge is different in this tribe called the kingdom of God. But there is a challenge for you today: will you be obedient to turn your life over to the authority of Jesus Christ? Will you say *I will live for You,* regardless? That is your life-long eternal immunity challenge. You may already be in a walk with God, but you're experiencing struggles and setbacks. You're under God's cloud of favor, but you've become distracted. Maybe you've become unmotivated or disinclined, and all you want to do is prop your feet up in front of the television and eat french fries. All you want to do is watch reruns, or Comedy Central, or HBO, and you've stopped wanting more of God. If that's you, I'm going to ask you a big question: Are you ready to turn that over to God? Are you ready to give that up to Him? Are you ready to say today that you will not be denied or disqualified? You've come too far, fought too hard, endured through too many challenges and you will *not* be disqualified by a moment of disinclination or distraction. You will not be disqualified by loving something that is outside of God's design. You will not lose your place for two bags of silver and two changes of clothes. You will not lose your future and your children's future over a moment of distraction.

Today, there it is: the big question. Are you willing to ask the big question? Are you ready? You are one difficult decision away from a brand new life! Will you face it and deal with it today? Today, can you give your life to Jesus Christ, the ultimate Survivor, who passed every test for you?

About the Author

---◆---

Dr. Bill Moore

Dr. Bill Moore has been in pastoral and evangelistic ministry since 1981. In 1985 he married his wife Anne and together they joined forces in the ministry. After planting several churches and extensive ministry work, they currently pastor Livingway Family Church a growing multi-campus church and Christian school.

Bill and Anne have three children Ryan, Marcus and Christopher and daughter-in-law Jacquey. Bill has also authored *Show Us The Father* and *Discovering Your Ministry Assignment*. Bill and Anne are now conducting Crusades all over the world. Their emphasis is equipping leaders and pastors to steward the end-time harves

PRAYER OF SALVATION

God loves you—no matter who you are, no matter what your past. God loves you so much that He gave His one and only begotten Son for you. The Bible tells us that "...whoever believes in him shall not perish but have eternal life" (John 3:16 NIV). Jesus laid down His life and rose again so that we could spend eternity with Him in heaven and experience His absolute best on earth. If you would like to receive Jesus into your life, say the following prayer out loud and mean it from your heart.

Heavenly Father, I come to You admitting that I am a sinner. Right now, I choose to turn away from sin, and I ask You to cleanse me of all unrighteousness. I believe that Your Son, Jesus, died on the cross to take away my sins. I also believe that He rose again from the dead so that I might be forgiven of my sins and made righteous through faith in Him. I call upon the name of Jesus Christ to be the Savior and Lord of my life. Jesus, I choose to follow You and ask that You fill me with the power of the Holy Spirit. I declare that right now I am a child of God. I am free from sin and full of the righteousness of God. I am saved in Jesus' name. Amen.

If you prayed this prayer to receive Jesus Christ as your Savior for the first time, please contact us on the Web at **www.harrisonhouse.com** to receive a free book.

Or you may write to us at

Harrison House • P.O. Box 35035 • Tulsa, Oklahoma 74153

The Harrison House Vision

Proclaiming the truth and the power

Of the Gospel of Jesus Christ

With excellence;

Challenging Christians to

Live victoriously,

Grow spiritually,

Know God intimately.